What People Are Saying About
Life Before the Internet

Michael Gentle has succeeded in writing a book that is neither an anti-tech rant nor a call for a return to some idyllic past. An entertaining read.

François Jolles, CIO, International Union for the Conservation of Nature, Switzerland

An insightful look at a slower and simpler time, and a reflection on what we have gained and lost. It raises some interesting questions on the effects of the internet on health and well-being in a digital age.

Lilian Dudley, Emeritus Associate Professor, Department of Global Health, Stellenbosch University, South Africa

Michael Gentle reminds us of some of the small pleasures of life, from enjoying an evening out without interruption to not having to work at home, much of which has been replaced by 24/7 connectivity. Perhaps this insightful and highly enjoyable work will encourage us to occasionally revisit the charm of former times, albeit without forfeiting the advantages that technology now offers.

Dr. Nancy L. Segal, Psychology Professor, California State University, Fullerton; Director, Twin Studies Center

Life Before the Internet

What we can learn from the good old days

Previous Books

The CRM Project Management Handbook (Kogan Page, 2002)
ISBN 978-0749438982

IT Success (Wiley, 2007)
ISBN 978-0-470-72441-5

An Introduction to IT Project Financials (Lulu, 2011)
ISBN 978-1445764054

Life Before the Internet

What we can learn from the good old days

Michael Gentle

BOOKS

Winchester, UK
Washington, USA

JOHN HUNT PUBLISHING

First published by O-Books, 2023
O-Books is an imprint of John Hunt Publishing Ltd., 3 East St., Alresford,
Hampshire SO24 9EE, UK
office@jhpbooks.com
www.johnhuntpublishing.com
www.o-books.com

For distributor details and how to order please visit the 'Ordering' section on our website.

Text copyright: Michael Gentle 2022

ISBN: 978 1 80341 388 4
978 1 80341 389 1 (ebook)
Library of Congress Control Number: 2022944855

A CIP catalogue record for this book is available from the British Library.

Design: Lapiz Digital Services

UK: Printed and bound by CPI Group (UK) Ltd, Croydon, CR0 4YY
Printed in North America by CPI GPS partners

The author of this book does not dispense medical advice or
prescribe the use of any technique as a form of treatment for
physical, emotional, or medical problems without the advice of a
physician, either directly or indirectly. The intent of the author
is only to offer information of a general nature to help you in
your quest for emotional and spiritual well-being. In the event
you use any of the information in this book for yourself, which is
your constitutional right, the author and the publisher assume no
responsibility for your actions.

We operate a distinctive and ethical publishing philosophy in
all areas of our business, from our global network of authors to
production and worldwide distribution.

Contents

INTRODUCTION   1

1 When Amazon was just a river   3
2 How on earth did they manage?   6

HOME   11

3 Children learned to fend for themselves   13
4 Children played with each other, not with phones   16
5 Children played for hours outdoors   19
6 People knew how to use their hands   22
7 Children had limited access to pornography   25
8 We would always answer the phone   28
9 It was okay to drop in unannounced   31
10 We took photos for ourselves, not for others   34

SCHOOL   39

11 We were good at mental arithmetic   41
12 We had good penmanship   45
13 We were good at remembering things   49

SOCIAL INTERACTION   51

14 People gave us their full attention   53
15 There were advantages to being unconnected   56
16 Phone conversations were private   59
17 We wrote letters   62
18 People could disagree and still be polite to
    each other   65
19 Relationships required socialization   68
20 People spoke to each other in restaurants   71

LEISURE   75

21 Reading books was part of everyday life   77
22 We knew how to read maps   80
23 Travel had the power to surprise   83
24 Movie plots were more creative   87

WORK   91

25 There was no email distraction   93
26 You couldn't take work home with you   96
27 There were lots of secretaries in the workplace   99

OTHER   103

28 Patience was part of everyday life   105
29 Physical activity was part of everyday life   108

IN CLOSING   111

30 Technostalgia   113
31 Off the grid in Mexico   116

APPENDIX   119

The internet made simple   121
Biography   127
Note to Reader   128
References   129
Further Reading   131

To Olivier

Acknowledgements

I would like to give special thanks to my brother, Robert, without whose valuable insight and editing, this book would not have seen the light of day.

I would also like to thank my son, Steven, for sharing his experiences off the grid while on holiday, which appears as a chapter in this book.

Thanks also to my son Kevin and my good friend Doris Edwards for their in-depth review of the manuscript.

And finally, thanks to John Hunt Publishers, whose highly streamlined proposal and production processes greatly simplified bringing this book to market.

INTRODUCTION

Chapter 1

When Amazon was just a river

I think the internet is one of the greatest inventions of all time, sitting right up there with the motor car and commercial air travel. As far as technology goes, it's clearly the greatest show on earth.

The internet has improved our lives beyond measure. We have a wealth of information at our fingertips that used to require a trip to the library. We are just a video call away from our loved ones on the other side of the world. Yesterday's products and services, which used to require paper forms and standing in line, have been reengineered to such an extent that what used to take days and weeks now takes hours and minutes. You can shop online from the comfort of your living room, and let your goods make the journey rather than you. You can rent out your home, your car – and even your clothes – to complete strangers.

The internet is now so much a part of our lives that it has become like electricity: it's always on, you don't care how it works or which power station it comes from, just so long as it's there.

Few people (starting with me) would wish to return to the predominantly paper-based era of the late 20th century. That would be like wishing to return to a time when there were no cars or airplanes.

And yet, much as we welcome these amazing benefits, the old way of life often hides positive aspects that we used to take for granted and that are now on the verge of being lost forever.

For example, the flexibility of working from home is clearly a huge advantage, but few would dispute the fact that we had better work-life balance back in the days when this was not possible. Parents may feel secure knowing that their children are always reachable, but there was a time when this just wasn't an option, so children had to learn to fend for themselves.

I came to the internet as an adult. I therefore belong to a generation that can talk about the era before the internet based not on research, but on actual experience. Author Michael Harris is another. As he says in his book, *The End of Absence*: "If we're the last people in history to know life before the internet, we are also the only ones who will ever speak, as it were, both languages. We are the only fluent translators of Before and After" (Michael Harris, 2014).

This is a book about Before and After.

I grew up in the 1960s, when Amazon was just a river, a domain was a stately home and to browse meant you were looking around. We didn't have a phone or even a television in our house until I was ten years old. We listened to the radio for entertainment. We played outdoors for hours on end. We read books to while away the time, or played board games like Monopoly and Scrabble.

When I was at university in the 1970s studying mechanical engineering, I did my calculations on a slide-rule, since affordable, hand-held electronic calculators only appeared towards the end of the decade. If you're wondering what a slide-rule is, it's a wooden contraption about the size of a big ruler that has two logarithmic scales that allow you to do multiplication and division. And if you're wondering what a logarithmic scale is, you probably weren't paying attention during maths class at school.

When I started working in the 1980s, the newly invented PCs and Macs of the computer revolution were still hugely expensive. So, the only high-tech device on an office desk was likely to be a push-button phone.

In the 1990s, I started using email and got my first laptop and cell phone (or mobile phone). In 2002, I became one of the early users of the Blackberry, well before the arrival of the iPhone five years later.

By the time the internet went mainstream at the turn of the century, I was 40 years old. My children were in their mid- to late teens and had also essentially grown up without the internet. Compared to today, we were a family of tech dinosaurs. Then again, so were millions of others.

The internet rapidly became an integral part of my work. As an IT professional, I quickly went native as I embraced the internet in all its wonder and complexity. I became as internet-savvy as the next person.

Today, in my sixties, and with considerably less hair, I have to say that it has been quite a ride – one that I would now like to share with you. You will see how the last unconnected generation used to live, and catch the tempo of everyday life, from home and family to work and leisure. You will come away with a fresh understanding of some of the unintended consequences of living in a hyper-connected society. And – who knows? – you might even decide to make some changes.

Chapter 2

How on earth did they manage?

Many digital natives probably wonder just how their parents and grandparents ever managed before the arrival of the internet. No email, no smartphones, no Google – everyday life must have been really hard!

Actually, it wasn't hard at all. It was easy. In fact, it was very high-tech. To understand how that's even possible, let's do a simple thought experiment.

Fast-forward to 2050, where we discover that teleportation is now possible, just like in *Star Trek* ("Beam me up, Scotty!"). Teleportation means that people can be transported anywhere in the world, with body, soul and luggage disappearing at, say, Frankfurt, and reappearing on the other side of the world in, say, Toronto. "Travel time" is virtually instantaneous.

Now also imagine that some author with time on his hands writes a mildly interesting book called *Life Before Teleportation: What we can learn from the good old days*. Readers would learn that back in the 2020s, you actually had to physically travel by plane to get from Frankfurt to Toronto, an 8-hour flight that would involve such unpleasant things as going through airport security, eating airline food and sitting in the middle seat for the whole journey.

The "teleportation natives" of 2050, who will never have seen the inside of a plane, would probably wonder how we even put up with such travel back then. The hassle, the onboard experience and the sheer waste of time is something they couldn't even imagine. "Thank goodness for teleportation," they would say. "How on earth did they manage?"

Today in the 2020s, your likely reaction is that we're managing just fine. Nobody is waiting impatiently for some futuristic technology to arrive to replace intercontinental air travel. Why, we're not even waiting for supersonic travel so that we can get there in half the time.

Another example: keyboards. Today's basic voice assistants will almost certainly evolve over the next ten years to the point where keyboards are no longer required to dialogue with a computer. And yet, when you use your computer today, do you curse your keyboard and yearn for full voice control? Of course not. You merrily type away because you live in the present. You know that your keyboard is the most advanced technology of its kind.

When you stop to think of it, hindsight comparisons are really just intellectual exercises in which people judge the past by the standards of the present. If nothing else, it is intellectually dishonest.

In a *New Scientist* article entitled "Clarke's Three Laws", we learn that the late science-fiction writer, Arthur C. Clarke, came up with what he saw as some fundamental truths – and you will no doubt recognize the third one:

- When a distinguished but elderly scientist states that something is possible, he is almost certainly right. When he states that something is impossible, he is very probably wrong.
- The only way of discovering the limits of the possible is to venture a little way past them into the impossible.
- Any sufficiently advanced technology is indistinguishable from magic.

Predicting what future technologies might look like runs into the above laws. You're effectively asking people to imagine things that would appear to be impossible, if not magical, by the standards of the day.

For example, I can't imagine a single person before the era of GPS satellite navigation saying, "I'm really tired of reading a map to get from point A to point B. Why can't somebody invent a talking car that tells me how to get there?"

Or someone waiting in line outside a phone booth saying, "This is such a waste of my time; when will someone invent a cordless pocket-phone so that I can call anyone, anytime, anywhere?"

These imaginary solutions would essentially be indistinguishable from magic. If any of our parents or grandparents had dared to imagine some of the internet-based technologies we have today, people would have laughed them out of the room and wondered just what they'd been smoking.

Today, you'd be hard-pressed to come up with a present-day technology that you think is terrible and imagine what it might look like in the future. Even science-fiction authors and movie scriptwriters – who certainly put a lot of effort into their predictions – get a few things surprisingly right, and a lot of things laughably wrong.

The original TV series *Star Trek*, for example, was – uncharacteristically – a pretty good predictor of the future, especially considering that it was created in the 1960s. The scriptwriters accurately foresaw things like mobile devices, Bluetooth headsets, tablet computers and voice-interface computers (and, who knows, maybe one day we'll add teleportation to the list).

On the other hand, 20 years later, the 1982 movie *Blade Runner* got a lot wrong when trying to imagine the year 2019. Its predictions of replicant humanoid robots and flying cars were hopelessly optimistic, to put it charitably. The movie was even incapable of predicting cell phones, which were only ten years away. Instead, the futuristic people of 2019 still used payphones (albeit with video screens) and paid by credit card.

As the baseball-playing philosopher, Yogi Berra, reportedly once said, "It's tough to make predictions, especially about the future."

At the end of the day, our minds are constrained by our current scientific knowledge – see again Clarke's first two laws. In other words, we don't know what we don't know. This explains why people are generally satisfied with whatever technology they're using. Every era is high-tech compared to the previous one; even the iron age was high-tech compared to the stone age. With the exception of visionary entrepreneurs like Elon Musk or Jeff Bezos, there are few frustrated people silently screaming, "There must be a better way!"

So next time you wonder just how your parents or grandparents managed before the internet, you can rest assured that they managed just fine – as fine as you and I are managing today with our current technologies, which will be hopelessly outdated by 2050.

HOME

Chapter 3

Children learned to fend for themselves

Before cell phones, smartphones and 24/7 connectivity, children left the house in the morning and often didn't see their parents again until the end of the day. Like the Apollo astronauts in radio silence on the far side of the moon, they were unreachable till they showed up again, and neither they nor their parents fretted about it.

This responsibility forced children to plan their day and deal with the vicissitudes of daily life, from missing the bus to running out of money. They had to improvise and make decisions. They acquired the autonomy and self-confidence necessary to become capable adults – the term in vogue at the time was "street-smart".

Children today might still grow up to be capable adults, but they are less able to fend for themselves because of the smartphone in their pocket. Not only can they call their parents at any time, but their parents can also call them – and that might well be worse. Perhaps this permanent digital umbilical cord isn't in everyone's best interests. Children may grow up to be less autonomous, and parents less trusting that their kids can make it through the day unaided.

Moms and dads today wave goodbye to their children as they set off on a short journey to the cinema or across town – and then add anxiously, "Text me when you get there." When did parents start concluding that their kids are basically incapable of getting from A to B in one piece?

How different it was for us free-range children of the pre-internet era. We were allowed to roam far from home without the constant worry that something might happen to us. That level of freedom today could get parents arrested.

I grew up in a safe and pleasant middle-class suburb with my twin brother. We were both roaming around in the street where we lived from as early as six years old, after having been taught the basics of road safety by adults and older children. Our parents would regularly send us to the corner shop to buy odds and ends. The store was just a few hundred yards away, on the intersection of a quiet suburban street. We always walked on the sidewalk facing oncoming traffic, just like we had been taught. We had learned the right way to cross a street – look left, right and left again, and walk across only once it's safe to do so. Monday to Friday, we went to school on our own using public transport, just like most of our classmates.

But it was on weekends that the real adventure started. With our friends from the neighbourhood, we would play football in the park, walk to the cinema several blocks away to catch a movie, or to the municipal swimming pool to mess around in the deep end – even though we had never been taught how to swim. And during it all, there was never a parent in sight. The very notion would have been laughable. Parents trusted their children not to do anything stupid and be home in time for dinner. It was a textbook definition of benign neglect.

This type of upbringing was the norm in much of the world. You only have to watch the sitcoms, cartoons and dramas of the time to notice that TV children were not constrained by parental angst. Like their real-life counterparts, they were mostly out of the house playing, getting up to mischief and riding their bicycles in the street.

Perhaps not surprisingly, I brought up my own children this way. By the age of ten, they would walk or cycle to their nearby school. They had no organized activities after school and were essentially left to their own devices. They were out playing somewhere: at the sports field, in the street or at someone's house.

Many modern parents probably worry that, unlike in the "good old days" before the internet, their children are at greater risk today of traffic accidents, child abduction and countless other dangers. However, all available research suggests exactly the opposite: the risks children face today are significantly less than they were thirty years ago. However, the perception is that they have increased, fuelled by sensational media reports and personal horror stories shared millions of times on social media. There was a time when ignorance was bliss. Thanks to the internet, this is no longer possible.

So-called helicopter parenting, characterized by excessive concern about children's safety, was a societal phenomenon that started to take root in the 1990s. It was greatly amplified soon afterwards with the arrival of mobile technology and the internet, which allowed parents to be permanently connected to their children – even to the extent of monitoring their location through geolocalization apps.

Fortunately, people are slowly starting to question the wisdom of constantly keeping tabs on kids and wrapping them in cottonwool. Leading the charge in the USA is Lenore Skenazy, who was labelled by the media as America's worst mom after she let her nine-year-old son ride the subway alone in New York and wrote a column about it. She fought back and started her Free-Range Kids movement. She is president of Let Grow, which promotes childhood independence and resilience, and is the author of the book, *Free-Range Kids: How Parents and Teachers Can Let Go and Let Grow*. Meanwhile, the state of Utah passed a bill in 2018 making it legal for parents to let their children go outside unsupervised – for example, to play in the park, go to the store or walk to school. Several other US states are said to be considering similar legislation.

As a popular quote puts it, a ship in port is safe, but that's not what ships are built for.

Chapter 4

Children played with each other, not with phones

Before smartphones and computers, children and teens rarely played alone. They were always doing things with other children, or with their parents. The notion of sitting alone in front of a screen, cut off from the world, would have seemed absurd. Games were eminently social in nature.

The first games I played as a child were with my mother at home, when I was barely five years old. She would challenge my brother and me to Pick Up Sticks. The game involved dropping a loose bunch of long, thin sticks onto a table into a random pile, and then trying to remove them one at a time without disturbing the others. When we got tired of that, she introduced us to card games like Old Maid, Snap and Happy Families. These indoor games were also commonly known as parlour games, which had their heyday during the Victorian Age in 19th-century England and kept ladies and gentlemen of leisure pleasurably occupied in their parlours.

It wasn't long before we moved on to board games such as Snakes and Ladders, and Ludo. We also did jigsaw puzzles and built things using Meccano sets – which, unlike Lego blocks, required the use of nuts, screws and bolts. My brother and I would play with each other or with other children in the neighbourhood. We were constantly in and out of each other's homes.

Around age eight or nine, our competitive drive had kicked in and we graduated to board games like Monopoly and the horse-racing game, Totopoly. We also started to play card games like gin rummy and Casino. It was now serious business, and you really went all out to win.

In our teens, we moved to more elaborate board games like draughts (checkers) and Scrabble. We learned how to professionally shuffle a pack of cards and were by now playing games like contract whist (similar to bridge), flush and poker.

Because we played with other children, there was a lot of chatting, joking and laughter, which contributed to bonding and social development. Sure, it felt good to win, but equally important was being together and having a good time.

All these different games taught you valuable social skills such as patience, waiting your turn and not hurrying others along. You also learned that cheating didn't pay, because sooner or later you would be caught out and maybe not invited to play again. So, you learned the value of enlightened self-interest long before you'd heard of the concept.

You also learned some life lessons without necessarily being aware of it – like not being a sore loser. You can't win every time. You tried to be graceful in defeat and perhaps magnanimous in victory – at least to the extent that this is possible when you're still a child who likes nothing more than to revel in the thrill of victory.

You also gained useful insights into notions of fairness and unfairness. On the one hand, it might seem unfair that one person wipes everyone else out in Monopoly and ends up getting all the money. On the other hand, it is very fair because all players have an equal chance of winning. Everyone starts out with the same amount of money, the same privileges and the same access to information. You learn that when things don't work out, it's not always somebody's fault – sometimes it's just the roll of the dice.

The digital games of today are completely different. There is no social element (even when played against others online) since the objective is to better one's score and move to the next level. Many of them are about movement, with often complex rules which can yield multiple – and sometimes infinite – outcomes based on one's cognitive skills and hand-eye coordination. It's doubtful whether there are any lasting life lessons to be learned when playing in this way against a computer.

That said, I'm a big fan of both. I love the socialization that comes with playing parlour games with friends and family; winning is almost secondary. But I also look forward to the thrill of improving my score and moving to the next level in the digital games that I play (I was an early addict of Tetris, and always had multiple Scrabble games active with online opponents around the world).

But the clear dominance of impersonal digital games over face-to-face parlour games means that today's children might be losing out in terms of social development.

There is also the very real danger of addiction to certain types of video games, something that is not associated with parlour games. Much as I love a session of Scrabble, Dixit or contract whist with friends, we call it a day after a few hours and stop for some fresh air, a drink and a chat. You could call it game-life balance.

Chapter 5

Children played for hours outdoors

The great indoors – now that would be funny if it weren't so true. Today's modern child in search of distraction is most likely to be found cooped up at home glued to a screen.

In pre-internet times, however, when children wanted to distract themselves, they went outside and did something physical like kicking a ball, playing hopscotch or riding a bike. If you were looking for one of your friends, they were almost certainly outside somewhere.

It even showed in the language you used when you knocked on the door. You typically said, "Good afternoon, Mrs Wilson – is Tom at home?" Alternatively, it might be, "Can Tom come out to play?" You hardly ever said, "Can I come in to see Tom?" That probably meant that he was sick in bed.

Before the internet, playing outdoors was natural. Running, jumping, climbing and falling down – it was all part of the rough-and-tumble of childhood. Not for nothing was the expression "to skin your knees" part of everyday vocabulary. Of course, children did sometimes stay indoors to play board games like Monopoly or Scrabble, but that was exceptional. Even poor weather was hardly a deterrent: there was nothing more enjoyable than running around in the rain or messing about in the snow.

My brother and I used to spend hours with our friends in the big park in our street, which had swings, see-saws, a jungle-gym, a sliding-board and a merry-go-round. We played football, cricket and tag there. We climbed trees, flew kites and played marbles.

When we needed a hard surface, we would simply play in a quiet street. The neighbourhood girls would play hopscotch or skip with their skipping ropes. We boys would roller-skate or push each other in makeshift carts made out of Coca-Cola crates and pram wheels. When we saw the odd car coming, we simply got out of the way and waited for it to pass. The street was very much a part of our playground.

It was during all this unorganized and unstructured outdoor play that we fine-tuned our motor skills, balance and agility. Without even being aware of it, we also developed our self-confidence and the ability to make decisions. We learned to take risks by doing ever more daring – and sometimes stupid – things. We learned what worked and what didn't (boy, did we try out things!). If you didn't yet know how to climb a tree, ride a bike or jump off the top of the jungle-gym, you learned it fairly quickly because your social standing in the group depended on it.

There were no signs anywhere warning us of the supposed dangers of climbing trees, jumping off swings or throwing things at each other, all of which we did with gleeful abandon. We were not warned that we were using the park at our own risk. Mercifully, the litigious society and the nanny state were still decades away, and the pleasures of outdoor play had not yet been curtailed by helicopter parents excessively concerned for their children's safety. In some countries (particularly the United States and England), this obsession would eventually lead to the gradual removal in parks and playgrounds of slides, merry-go-rounds and jungle-gyms, for fear that children might hurt themselves, potentially triggering a lawsuit. How tragicomic it is that when pre-internet children hurt themselves while playing, it was part of growing up; today it has become somebody else's fault.

Thanks to all this unstructured and unsupervised physical activity, we also learned to play a wide range of sports with little or no formal training. We mainly learned from each other, and by watching older children play. By the time we got to high school, we were pretty decent at most ball games, and could put in a fairly creditable performance on the athletics field.

Today, however, sport for children is often formal and structured, complete with training and coaching. They typically specialize in just one or two disciplines – say, football or tennis. It's less about having fun and more about improving one's game. It's rare to find many twelve-year-olds today who are comfortable across a wide range of different sports, because they rarely had the benefit of lots of unstructured outdoor play during childhood.

Today's internet children spend far less time playing outdoors than their parents did at the same age, with a corresponding impact on their health, motor skills and social development. There are only around five hours of daylight time left after school, and much of this is spent in front of screens.

Until a new mindset emerges among all parties – parents, educators and the children themselves – that playing outside is an essential part of growing up, the lure of the screen will continue to prove irresistible.

Chapter 6

People knew how to use their hands

In today's electronic age, people use their hands mainly to press, point, swipe, click and scroll. But in the days before screens and keyboards, people used their hands to do things and fix stuff. And for good reason – they lived in what was essentially a mechanical age.

Things were built with components that people could generally understand, such as springs, gears, circuits, nuts and bolts. They were made with everyday materials like metal, wood, glass and leather. So, when they broke down, they weren't thrown away; they were repaired. Far more things were repaired back then compared to today, from radios and TVs to cameras and watches. Even shoes were repaired and resoled. Repair shops were very much part of the neighbourhood, and you found them on every street corner. Even though products cost much less in absolute terms than they do today, people had to work proportionately more hours to be able to afford them. So, it made financial sense to try to repair things yourself first. And that meant using your hands.

Take cars. Back then, they weren't crammed with complex electronics like they are today. People tinkered around and did their own minor repairs. When I was growing up, taking the family car in for a regular service was an alien concept. Time to change the oil, replace the air filter and check the spark plugs? You did that yourself. My brother and I used to change the oil in our parents' car from the age of twelve.

Children would regularly see their fathers or older brothers replace a flat tyre. It was a basic skill you picked up very early in life, and certainly by the time you left high school. After all, what kind of girl would want to go out with you if you couldn't even change a flat tyre by the roadside?!

Manual dexterity was something you acquired at an early age. We did woodwork at school and were taught how to use tools like saws, chisels and planes. In fact, it was a subject my father taught, alongside technical drawing. I still remember my first wooden locomotive that I made at school at the age of ten. I was so proud of it!

In our neighbourhood, children usually had access to some parent's garage or den. It would have a workbench and a wide variety of materials and tools like wood, bamboo, paper, metal, glue, string, scissors, hammers, nails and saws. It was also relatively easy to scavenge items like pram wheels, ball bearings, planks and crates. For example, we used to build rudimentary carts and scooters using Coca-Cola crates for the frame, and ball bearings for wheels. We also made our own catapults, and bows and arrows, using sticks and branches from the trees in the neighbourhood. We even built our own kites. All you needed was string, a lozenge-shaped bamboo frame, special kite paper and good-quality glue. Expertise was crowd-sourced: there was always someone, somewhere, who knew more than you. We all learned from each other.

This way of life has since disappeared with the advent of sophisticated electronics, increased product reliability and lower prices. So, when modern consumer devices break down and the guarantee period is over, it may make economic sense to just buy a new one. Most products, from cameras to cars, are so crammed with complex electronics anyway, hidden away behind inaccessible plastic casings, that you have zero chance of fixing anything yourself. If your car broke down on the side of the road thirty years ago, a mechanic would come along with his toolbox; today, he'd come with a laptop and a diagnostic kit.

Another thing my father taught us to do in the home from an early age was to change faulty plugs and fuses on our electrical appliances, particularly lamps, the kettle and the toaster. Today, you'd have to go onto YouTube to learn how to do this (assuming you'd even need to). Meanwhile, my mother patched holes in our socks and shirts, sewed on buttons, and adjusted the hem on trousers and skirts. She often knitted jerseys for us instead of buying them in a department store. Just as boys were taught woodwork at school, girls were taught needlework. These were basic household and survival skills, probably the equivalent today of everyday computer skills.

Today, unless you actually use your hands for a living – for example as a chef or a plumber – the closest you'll probably get to manual work is assembling furniture from Ikea!

A personal anecdote illustrates this well. One Sunday morning about twenty years ago, I had a flat tyre outside our house in suburban Paris. It was a weekend, the sun was shining and I had the time. So, rather than call Roadside Assistance, I decided to change the wheel myself. I called my teenage children to come and see how it was done. I'll always remember how astonished they were that I was able to do it myself ("Wow, Dad, you mean you know how to change a tyre?!"). They found the whole operation quite fascinating, especially as I got them to participate and learn how to use a jack and a wheel-brace. Prior to that, I hadn't changed a wheel in over twenty years. But it's like riding a bicycle – it's something you never forget.

Chapter 7

Children had limited access to pornography

I saw my first *Playboy* magazine in high school when I was twelve years old, and it would be more than a decade later before I even had the opportunity to see a pornographic film. By today's standards of instant, wall-to-wall pornography, this almost certainly qualifies as arrested development – or maybe not, given the dangers of exposure to porn in children.

Pornography, in the sense of sexually explicit material intended to stimulate, is as old as humanity itself. But until the mid-20th century, reading or viewing it was illegal in many countries – for example, in my native South Africa, where I grew up. And even when it was not illegal, the social mores of the time essentially restricted its circulation. So, even though pornography ran the gamut from nude pictures and evocative soft porn to explicit hard-core material, its consumption remained an essentially hidden practice.

In the days before the internet, gaining access to pornography involved time, money and effort. You physically had to leave your home to find it. And you had to shell out big bucks for it: cheap thrills it definitely wasn't.

If you wanted a soft-core magazine like *Playboy*, for example, you would go to a local newsagent, preferably at night and in a neighbourhood where nobody knew you. It's not hard to imagine what happens next.

You would head to the magazine racks and pretend to be leafing through the latest copies of *Time* or *Newsweek*. Then, when you were sure nobody was looking, you would take your copy of *Playboy* from the top shelf and quickly go to the counter to pay for it. You would ask for a copy of the evening newspaper, too. You would avoid making eye contact with the sales assistant – especially if it was a woman – hand your money over and not linger in case somebody you knew saw you. You'd then hide your *Playboy* in the folds of the evening newspaper and stroll out, breathing a sigh of relief.

If you had even the slightest shred of middle-class decency and bought into the strict moral codes of the day, your heart would be pounding and your cheeks burning with shame. It was a mortifying experience for many, surpassed perhaps only by that of walking into a chemist to buy a pack of condoms – a scene played for laughs in countless movies and sitcoms, reminding us of a time when condoms weren't yet openly available on supermarket shelves and on wall dispensers in public toilets.

One can only imagine how much harder it must have been to go into a real porn shop, or to slink into a porn cinema and buy a ticket to view an X-rated movie. The patrons of these establishments were sometimes known as the "raincoat and sunglasses set", a reference to the extreme lengths they would go to avoid being recognized. Such hard-core porn outlets and cinemas were off-limits for children. If you weren't eighteen years old, or at least looked it, you had no chance of getting in. That alone was enough to keep you at home doing your homework or watching TV with the family.

Children therefore had limited access to porn in the pre-internet era. And even if they did somehow manage to find ways around the restrictions of the time, and had enough money, they were never going to see much of it anyway. It was always going to be a treat, an unusual event, a fantasy world not to be mistaken for reality.

Then in the 1980s something significant came onto the market – the VCR (Video Cassette Recorder). It ushered in the era of video rental, and the ability to view porn in the privacy of one's own home.

You could now go to the local video store and walk down the aisles, pretending to be looking for the latest Disney movie. Then, when you were sure nobody was watching, you could nonchalantly make your way over to the adult section. You'd sandwich your X-rated video between a couple of non-threatening films when you got to the till. The shame factor was still there, but to a lesser extent, because society was becoming a lot more tolerant and accepting of sex and nudity in the public domain.

It wasn't long before mainstream bookshops were stocking erotic literature in full view, cable and satellite television started offering porn channels alongside their traditional movie channels, and hotels started piping porn movies into their rooms. I can still remember my first European business trips in the 1980s, when I viewed porn movies for the first time – out of curiosity, naturally. The shame factor still made an appearance, this time when you checked out and were asked – often in a low voice – whether you had consumed any "in-room entertainment" during your stay. Ahem.

Today with the internet, there are no more barriers to porn. It's out in the public domain and pretty much in your face, accessible to anyone with ten functioning fingers. It's almost too easy. For many teens still struggling to navigate their emotional and hormonal selves through adolescence, it has become the norm. It distorts young people's view of male-female relationships, normalizes the sexual behaviour shown on-screen and creates unreasonable expectations of what a sexual life should be like.

I'm no prude – after all, I lived in France for most of my life – but I'm glad that I grew up during a more innocent time when pornography was a word I couldn't even spell, and the height of titillation was ogling the underwear ads in women's magazines and the lingerie models in home catalogues.

Chapter 8

We would always answer the phone

If you were at home right now and somebody knocked on your door, it's virtually certain that you'd get up to open it – or at the very least peer through the peephole to see who it was. It would never occur to you to say, "Ah, what the hell, let them knock. If it's important enough, they can slip a note under the door."

Yet that's exactly what many of us do today when our phone rings. Unless we're expecting a call, we'll have a quick look at the screen to see who it's from. If it's not a number or name that we recognize, we let it ring and go to voicemail. We can always check later, or even ignore it.

Our decision to let the phone ring and go to voicemail is entirely understandable in an age of telemarketing and social screening. And given that most people today prefer text messaging to phone calls anyway, it's even more likely that an unknown number is someone you'd rather not talk to, or somebody trying to sell you something.

How different it all was when I was growing up. We *always* answered the phone. It was like answering the door. Phones were expensive. Not everybody had one. Phone calls weren't cheap, especially if you were calling from a payphone. And there were no affordable answering machines or voicemail as we know it today. So, if somebody had taken the trouble to call you, then it was probably something important. You therefore gave them the courtesy of your attention. Repeatedly not answering the phone meant you were out of town – or worse, maybe lying dead on the kitchen floor.

The same was true at work. Before the generalization of digital caller displays on office phones in the 1990s (which allowed you to see the incoming name or number) you had no way of knowing who was calling. So, you answered the phone. After all, you didn't want to miss a call from a colleague, customer or supplier.

Even the way you answered the phone spoke to its importance as a means of communication. It wasn't just "Hello" or "Yeah?", but perhaps, "Good morning, Smith residence."

In today's modern age when just about everybody has a phone – even the homeless – and people routinely make video calls, it's hard to imagine just how unusual and special this instrument was just a few decades ago.

In the street where I grew up in the 1960s, most households did not have a phone. And yet, ours was a middle-class suburb where parents worked, owned their own homes and drove cars. My aunt who lived down the road had a phone, and it took pride of place in the living room. It was almost a status symbol. You always stopped what you were doing whenever it rang (which wasn't very often), because it seemed like such a special occasion. You waited to see who it was before carrying on with whatever you were doing.

Phones seemed totally unnecessary at the time, and we got along just fine without them. The same was true in most developed countries. In England, for example, figures from *Statista* show that in 1970, barely one household in three had a landline phone; by the mid-1990s, that number had shot up to nine households in ten. Not long afterwards, increasingly affordable cell phones started hitting the market, bringing phone ownership within reach of even poor people. Today, more than 90% of people in the world own a cell phone – and many no longer even bother installing a landline at home.

Even when you did have a phone in your home back then, calling someone wasn't exactly cheap. Calls were kept short and usually limited to the reason for the call – can you pick me up after work, or do you want to go to the movies tonight? Unless you were rich, or someone else was paying, you were unlikely to call someone just to shoot the breeze.

In an article in *The Conversation* entitled "Rise and fall of the landline: 143 years of telephones becoming more accessible", we learn that in 1968, the cost of a 3-minute call from New York to San Francisco was nearly $2 – or around $12 in today's money. By the early 2000s, long-distance call rates had fallen so low (to 6 cents per minute) that the Federal Communications Commission simply stopped bothering to track them.

It wasn't an unalloyed blessing, though. Cheap phone calls, coupled with the increasing sophistication of call centres and telephone systems, also meant an explosion in unwanted, nuisance calls from telemarketers trying to sell you stuff. Fortunately, at about the same time, affordable answering machines and voicemail systems finally started to go mainstream. So, we no longer had to take the call if we didn't want to – a practice that has since become the norm.

Chapter 9

It was okay to drop in unannounced

It would be unthinkable today to go around to someone's home and simply drop in unannounced without first texting or phoning; that would be the height of intrusiveness. But before the internet and cell phones, dropping in on friends and family was the norm.

In fact, the very concept of dropping in unannounced was a contradiction in terms and not even part of one's vocabulary. After all, what were you going to do – write a letter to fix an appointment? Make a phone call to say you were on your way over? Most households didn't even have a phone. And even then, the relatively high cost of phone calls was a deterrent. Your fingers didn't do the walking; you did.

In short, calling ahead before a visit just wasn't part of the culture. You would just turn up at someone's place, either alone or with friends, and you would usually find them home. Before long, you'd be chatting over tea, coffee or drinks in the lounge, or sprawled on the floor in the bedroom listening to music or playing a board game.

In the neighbourhood where I grew up, my brother and I were constantly in and out of friends' homes, and they were constantly in and out of ours. Often, front doors were just left open with a hook that fitted into an eye-latch on the wall. Of course, etiquette demanded that we still knock on the door or ring the doorbell and wait for someone to answer, but the subliminal message was unmistakeable – come right in!

Of course, not all visits were welcome, either in terms of the person visiting ("Oh, no – not them again!") or the time ("Oh, please, not now!"), but you dealt with it. People were usually savvy enough to read the signs and know when to gracefully cut short an inconvenient visit. My mother was particularly strict around mealtimes, and she hated it when anyone dared to drop in when we were about to sit down to eat.

In general, visitors were always welcome in our neighbourhood. In an age before text messages, cheap phone calls and video chats, it was how we maintained our social relationships. The familiar car pulling into the driveway, or the doorbell ringing, meant that you had company, and you showed your hospitality accordingly. Depending on who it was, you offered them a beer or a glass of wine, an assortment of snacks, or perhaps just tea and cake.

Sometimes, the knock on the door was just that of a child looking for company ("Hello, Mrs Hardy, can Jenny come out and play?"). This would either result in an invitation to step inside ("She's in her room. Come right in. Jennyyyy! Someone for you!") or an indication of where she might be ("She went out with Alice an hour ago, but I don't know where.").

Kids also knocked on doors when they were trying to find a friend or sibling. If a parent told you to "go and find your brother; he should have been back by now!", that meant going to the places where he was most likely to be. It could mean the park, the football field or a friend's place. That might mean knocking on a number of doors with a standard, "Good afternoon, is my brother here by any chance?" We sure did a lot of walking back then. Today, you'd just send a text message saying: "Where the heck are you?!"

Eventually, we left our childhood neighbourhood in Cape Town and moved to Lusaka, Zambia, where we lived our teen years in the 1970s. Our family had a phone by then – which was such a novelty that I still remember the number today, more than 50 years on! But we all still tended to drop in unannounced at each other's places because that was what we were used to. My mom and dad would probably have been offended if anyone had dared to phone first to ask if they could come around. After all, it was a social visit, not a doctor's appointment.

Even today, despite the convenience of cell phones, the habit of dropping in unannounced is so ingrained in me that I still occasionally give in to it. When my brother and I fly to Cape Town for a holiday, we sometimes drive to the homes of friends and family and just knock on the door and surprise them. The look on their faces is always priceless.

"Oh, my God! Look who it is? When did you two get in?"

Hugs, kisses, followed by tea and cake. Some things stay the same, despite the internet.

Chapter 10

We took photos for ourselves, not for others

Today, we live in an age of photo vanity where we share flattering pictures of the most mundane aspects of our lives with our friends, family and social-media connections. The perfect smile, the perfect outfit, the perfect background: these pictures, often filtered and photoshopped to within an inch of their lives, all seem to send a clear message to the world – look how great my life is!

This social one-upmanship is possible because virtually everyone has a camera-phone. Photos are easy to take, and they can be sent to others at the tap of a finger. Best of all, it costs so little that it's practically free.

Even I have been sucked in. Not so long ago, I would roll my eyes at the sight of people in restaurants taking photographs of their food to share with their friends. Now, I often find myself doing the same thing. When I discover a particularly interesting dish or a new restaurant, I might take a photo and send it to my twin brother, who lives thousands of miles away. And he would respond with a "bon appétit"!

It wasn't always like this.

Before the digital age, cameras were cumbersome and expensive, and the cost of photos kept your photographic zeal firmly in check.

A camera was a standalone instrument that was not part of some other device. You would usually carry it around your neck or over your shoulder. And the better the camera, the bigger and heavier it was. You just never saw people walking around with cameras unless they were tourists or press photographers. There was therefore no such thing as a spontaneous, everyday photo. Photography was something functional and private.

You only took pictures at special family occasions like birthday parties and weddings, or when you went on vacation.

Photos were a big deal, and you preserved these precious memories in a photo album. This was a physical, hardcover book with transparent sheeting designed to hold the photos in place without curling at the edges. Apart from family members and your closest friends, nobody ever saw your photo albums. The average family probably never took more than one or two hundred photos a year – ours certainly didn't – and only a very small proportion of those would find their way into an album.

This embarrassingly low level of photographic activity was perfectly understandable due to the cost, time and effort involved.

At the low end, there were basic, inexpensive point-and-shoot cameras for outdoor pictures of people, events and holidays. They required no technical knowledge; all you had to do was pop in a roll of film and start snapping. The first such camera was the Kodak Instamatic, which came out in the 1960s, and made home photography affordable for millions of people, including our family.

If you wanted a better-quality image, you had to move up-market to the more sophisticated Japanese reflex cameras from the likes of Nikon, Pentax or Olympus. These precision instruments came with a corresponding price tag. By the time you added in accessories like a flash, a pouch, a collapsible tripod, a light-meter and an over-the-shoulder carrier bag, you were easily looking at few hundred dollars or more.

Then you had to know how to combine the various camera settings to produce a quality picture. This was a learning experience that could take months.

Your next obstacle was the cost of film. Just as you first have to buy a toner cartridge before you can use your printer, you first had to buy a roll of film and load it into your camera before you could start using it. The most popular sizes were 24 and 36 exposures, which allowed you to take either 24 or 36 photos. Because your pictures were captured on a roll of film and not instantly on a screen, it was hard to take the "perfect" photo. It's why so many family photos of the time were terrible in terms of lighting, framing and embarrassing facial expressions.

Needless to say, you would be very selective about what you chose to photograph. Imagine you were on vacation in, say, Sydney, Australia. Ten shots of the Opera House from different angles? Forget it. Take two or three and move on.

Once you used up your roll of film, you'd carefully remove it from your camera and take it to a photo-processing lab to be developed into actual pictures. It could easily cost several dollars, and you'd still have to wait a few days before your finished photos were ready.

The big moment would finally arrive when you had your pictures. Breathlessly, you would go through them one by one, reliving the special moments that you had captured. This was usually a special occasion at home, celebrated around a table with the family, over coffee or a glass of wine. Laughter, fond reminiscing and groans of frustration over those photos that were so terrible they were not even worth keeping.

But it wasn't over yet. You then had to decide which of the photographs were worth making copies of, perhaps to send to friends and other family members. Finally, you went all the way back to the photo-processing lab with the negatives so that you could have the copies made.

So, all in all, personal photography was expensive and time-consuming before the age of the internet and the smartphone.

People who are familiar with both digital and analogue photography would probably agree that there is far more emotional value and personal investment in an original, untouched print photo than in a hundred digital pictures of the same scene, no matter how much photoshopping or filters you apply. When a photo requires time to get right and comes with a cost, you put a lot more thought and effort into taking one. Perhaps that's why photographs were so much more appreciated and valued back then compared to today's world of photographic hyperinflation.

The emotional value of actual photos is never more starkly illustrated than in movies. When you have a scene of someone shedding a tear or looking wistfully at the picture of a loved one, you can be sure it will be a print photo. I have yet to see such a scene played out using a digital photo on a screen.

Print photos are timeless.

SCHOOL

Chapter 11

We were good at mental arithmetic

Quick – what's 25% of 32? If it takes you more than three seconds to figure it out, then you probably grew up with the internet. Just as 50% is a half, 25% is a quarter, or ¼. So, all you have to do is divide 32 by 4, and the answer is 8. QED – quite easily done.

Today, thanks to electronic calculators, you can get the answer immediately on your phone. Does that mean that you know – and really understand – the answer? Not necessarily. It just means that you know how to find it.

In today's digital world, people have become experts at retrieving information. Fifty years ago, you needed to have much of that information at your fingertips in order to function.

Basic numeracy was part of the core skills that children had to learn at school. The other two were reading and writing, hence the term "the 3 Rs" – reading, writing and arithmetic ('rithmetic). Addition, subtraction, fractions, multiplication, short division, long division – these were basic computational skills that were drilled into us at primary school when we were barely eight years old. We spent hours repeating multiplication tables. We did endless class exercises. The teacher would call out random calculations (for example 12 times 9), and we had to give the answer immediately, the objective being instant recall rather than the ability to work it out.

It was classic rote learning – doing something over and over until it stuck. It was like listening to your favourite song and singing it over and over until you knew the lyrics by heart. That's why I know for sure that 12 times 9 is 108, just as I know, word for word, the lyrics of my favourite childhood songs. Both were being indelibly imprinted onto my brain through constant repetition – though the latter was far more pleasurable than the former!

This rigidly enforced intellectual discipline might seem cruel to today's generation, but there was a hard-nosed logic to it. In an age before electronic calculators and Google, if you didn't know how to do basic, everyday computation in your head, you couldn't function effectively in the world. How would you balance a chequebook? Estimate how far you could still travel in your car before the next service was due? Or work out the price on the dress in the window marked down by 40%? In fact, you might get the wrong change from a sales assistant and never know it.

In my early teens, I was part of a group of students who used to work in the school tuck-shop during the morning break. There was no cash register. Electronic calculators hadn't been invented yet, so we did everything in our heads. A typical order might be, "Two cokes, two Chelsea buns and a Kit-Kat chocolate." That was $2 \times 5 + 2 \times 3 + 1 \times 8 = 24$ cents (money went a long way back then). We handled dozens of such orders during the half-hour break. Only if it was a particularly large order would we resort to pencil and paper.

In restaurants, people were able to verify at a glance the handwritten bill and mentally split it among the guests if required – even after a few drinks!

Over the course of many planning meetings, strategy sessions and workshops during my long corporate career, I have noticed that people with good basic numeracy are more effective in grasping the big picture, and spotting trends and anomalies. That's because all the numbers being thrown around and the extent to which they may be changing – for example, the various costs of a project – can instantly be quantified and imbued with meaning. This, in turn, brings forth likely explanations and possible solutions. You don't have to call up the calculator on your smartphone. You can see the arithmetic landscape in your mind's eye, and not even Google will help you with that.

Poor numeracy in the workplace is a critical problem in many advanced economies, costing billions of dollars a year in lost productivity, according to various studies. A 2017 report by *Future of Earth*, entitled "Poor Numeracy Hits Workplace Productivity", notes that barely a quarter of British adults polled – that's one in four, or 25% – were able to work out a simple percentage increase in hourly pay rates, the interest on a savings account or how to convert pounds to dollars.

The poor understanding of percentages by the general population was on full display during the Covid pandemic, especially on TV news bulletins. For example, if the number of people infected increased by 1,250 from yesterday's count of 115,075, that might seem like a lot in absolute terms ("over a thousand!"), but it's only a 1% change. Conversely, an increase of 24 deaths from yesterday's count of 243 might seem small ("only" 24), but that represents 10%, which is far more worrying. It's not clear whether the media presented the information like this because they reckoned most viewers don't understand percentages, or whether they themselves don't understand it either. In any event, it wasn't helpful in explaining the big picture.

Poor numerical skills can also affect basic decisions in the home. I personally know of successful professionals – all university graduates – who don't know how to estimate the number of square feet of carpet to buy for a room, or how to take a recipe for four people and proportionately adjust the ingredient quantities for a larger group of six. To which they might justifiably retort – so what? And they'd be right. Poor numeracy doesn't prevent them from leading happy and fulfilled lives.

With calculators on our smartphones and computers, mental arithmetic no longer has the same importance as it once did. Whether that's a good or a bad thing is an ongoing debate, with compelling arguments on both sides.

For my part, I absolutely loved calculators when they first started appearing in the 1970s. I still remember the first one I bought, a Casio Fx-19. It tremendously simplified my engineering studies at university. However, I only ever used it for heavy-duty number-crunching. To this day, I still use my head for basic day-to-day computations.

Even today in the 2020s, I still see wizened old ladies at town and village markets in Europe nonchalantly totalling up purchases with pencil and paper.

Old habits die hard.

Chapter 12

We had good penmanship

Penmanship – now there's a word you hardly ever hear these days. It is defined as the art or skill of writing by hand using a pen or pencil. The result is your handwriting, which can look neat and elegant, or, if you have lousy penmanship, messy and hard to read.

Writing with a pen or pencil is one of the first fundamental skills that children learn at school. However, it was far more important before the screen-based technology of the internet, because paper was the primary means of collecting and sharing information.

There were very few occupations that did not require you to write things down. Office workers, waiters, store clerks, teachers, construction workers, you name it – they were all busy taking orders, drafting reports, filling in forms, or noting down the time of the next train. Your hand was never far away from a pen. People spent hours each day writing.

Right now, I am writing these words on a keyboard using Microsoft Word. In the pre-internet era of fifty years ago, I would have been using a pen and paper.

Authors typically wrote their books by hand – or longhand, to use the technically correct term – unless they preferred to type using a typewriter. Not all of them did. If you're up to speed with your internet trivia about J.K. Rowling, author of the bestselling *Harry Potter* series, you'll know that she wrote her first book by hand in 1994 using pen and paper, while sitting in a café with her infant daughter asleep next to her. It's an approach she apparently still uses, and only afterwards does she transfer her work to computer. Several other famous writers are said to use this approach too, including Danielle Steel and Stephen King.

With writing being such an important part of your life, you had to be able to write fast. Children therefore learned joined-up (or cursive) writing at school. It means the pen never leaves the page while you write a word, because all the individual letters are joined up. The pen glides across the paper in a smooth, fluid movement. The result is you write much faster.

Writing fast was one thing; you also had to be able to write neatly, or at least legibly, so that people could decipher your writing. That's where good penmanship came in. A fine and flowing handwriting was far more desirable than a thick, disorderly scribble. We had handwriting classes at school, and our teachers taught us how to write properly ("thin upstrokes, thick downstrokes"). We had weekly handwriting tests, which were graded "poor", "good" or "very good". My handwriting was rather average, and only once did I ever get a "very good".

Rightly or wrongly, people would form a first impression of you based on your handwriting style. This became particularly important when applying for a job. Your handwriting style was believed to reflect aspects of your character, an area of science – or pseudoscience, depending on your view – known as graphology. When I applied for my first job in Paris after graduating from university in the early 1980s, I knew that my handwriting was going to be analyzed by a professional graphologist. This was standard practice at the time in France, and companies insisted on handwritten job applications. Whatever my handwriting revealed, I'll never know, but I got the job.

The brand and type of pen that you used were important clues to your social status. A ballpoint pen was cheap and practical, while a fountain pen – which came with its own refillable ink cartridge – was both expensive and elegant. Pens were probably one of the first status symbols. Pen envy was part of growing up. Indeed, when it came to birthday and Christmas presents, you couldn't go wrong with an expensive, brand-name pen: for example, a Parker.

During my early school years, boys and girls would often come to class with a snazzy new fountain pen equipped with a clever mechanism for replenishing the ink. After the many stares of admiration, the more daring among us would then ask if we could try it out.

"Wow – it writes really smoothly!"

"That's enough – you're using up my ink!"

Good penmanship was also important in the workplace, which was overwhelmingly paper-based. Your handwriting was on full display among colleagues, secretaries and management. Good handwriting was part and parcel of one's professionalism at work.

Today, in an age of keyboards and voice-recognition software, people hardly write anymore. When they do, it's rarely more than a few lines. And for those who never learned to write in cursive, it's maddeningly slow. The result can be a level of penmanship and writing speed that would embarrass a ten-year-old from the pre-internet era. If you attend workplace meetings where people of widely differing ages are present, you might notice how more easily and fluidly the "oldies" are able to take notes.

Which is better – pen or keyboard? Has penmanship now been replaced by, er, screenmanship?

Interestingly, research suggests that we process and retain information better when we write it by hand. Try writing your name with pen and paper. Now type it on a keyboard; it just doesn't feel the same. Indeed, cursive writing is said to help children in their motor development, and even set the brain up for cognitive development. It apparently also leads to easier recall when learning to read – and especially when learning a foreign language, something that I can personally attest to.

Nevertheless, many countries have stopped teaching children cursive writing at school. In the United States, it is no longer mandatory, and is decided at state level. Even Finland, that bastion of progressive education and academic excellence, did away with it in 2015.

Good penmanship remains a much-debated issue in academic circles. Like that of numeracy, it shows that the benefits of the internet have been overshadowed by the loss of certain basic skills that society once deemed important.

Chapter 13

We were good at remembering things

Before the internet allowed us to recall essential information at the click of a mouse, people had to keep it in their heads. This meant lots of rote learning and memorization, so they became unusually good at retaining and recalling information.

The brain has often been likened to a muscle, in that the more you use it for a given task, the stronger it gets and the easier the task becomes. For example, in order to be licensed, London black-cab drivers spend two years or more memorizing every street and landmark around the centre of the city. Researchers have found that the part of the brain used to perform this task – the hippocampus – is markedly bigger in these drivers than in the average person.

Today, with a smartphone in every pocket, there's not much pressure any longer to remember facts and figures. You need someone's phone number? Go to your Contacts list. You want to know what time your friend's flight is landing at the airport? Google arrivals and departures. How do you convert inches to centimetres? Just call up the conversion algorithm.

Who needs to be smart when you have a smartphone? But back in the pre-internet era when paper was king, it was a different story.

People knew key phone numbers by heart. They knew the main times of their buses or trains without ever having to look at the timetable. Remembering stuff wasn't the exception; it was the norm.

As a university student in France, navigating the Paris metro and suburban train lines was something I had to do every day to get to classes, go to the movies or visit friends. Within barely a few weeks, I knew by heart which trains to take, where to change stations and the departure times – right down to the minute – of the most important trains. It was a basic mental competence that practically all users of public transport possessed.

The same logic applied to phone numbers and addresses. I had to recall them so often, especially when filling in forms, that they became indelibly imprinted in my brain. Today, fifty years on, I can still remember some of the addresses and phone numbers from my childhood and early teens, even though I no longer have any use for them. But I would be hard-pressed to remember my last home address and phone number from a few years ago. Then again, I no longer need to, because it will show up somewhere in a pre-populated form online.

People were also good at general knowledge, simply because they had to learn such a lot of it at school. From the dates of key events in history to the great rivers and cities of the world, we had it all at our fingertips. Today, on TV game shows, you sometimes see contestants struggling with basic general-knowledge questions ("What's the largest ocean in the world?") that any twelve-year-old could have answered a generation ago.

When I wake up in the middle of the night and have trouble falling asleep, I don't count sheep (do people actually do that?!). Rather, I run through cities in the world from A-Z, or the weather areas of the Shipping Forecast on BBC radio. The regular repetition ensures easy recall, and within five to ten minutes, I am fast asleep again.

In the days before the internet, a good working memory was quite normal. It wasn't that we were necessarily smarter than today's generation; it's just that we had to remember stuff, so we became good at it.

SOCIAL INTERACTION

Chapter 14

People gave us their full attention

Give me your undivided attention.

There was a time, before smartphones and the internet, when you rarely ever had to say this. It went without saying that when you sat down to interact socially with someone, you would usually have their full attention. And if for whatever reason you only had their partial attention, even that was a lot because your conversation was unlikely to be stopped in mid-sentence. The only way a family conversation could be interrupted was if the phone rang, or someone knocked at the door. At work, if a person's office door was closed and their phone forwarded to voicemail, then they were unlikely to be interrupted.

And a restaurant was the one place where you were virtually guaranteed people's full attention because it was impossible to be interrupted – except, of course, by the waiter coming round to ask if everything was okay.

Undivided attention is unfortunately no longer possible. It is divided between you and your smartphone – and maybe even the laptop standing open on your desk.

When I sit down to talk with someone, whether in a business or a social setting, and they put their phone on the table in front of them – even when it's on silent – the signal they're sending me is clear: they might answer it or, at the very least, glance at the screen.

Next time you're at a conference presentation with a hundred or more people in the audience, take a look around you. It's a fair bet that most people will be dividing their time between the presenter and their phone. Even panellists on stage will at times look at their phone. Interestingly enough, if these very same people opened a laptop instead and started typing away, it would be considered extremely rude. But with a phone, it's somehow acceptable.

We've reached the stage where answering your phone or checking a text in mid-meeting is not even considered impolite anymore. Indeed, the contrary might be the case – how can you *not* take the call or check the text message? After all, it might be important.

Such interruptions have been popularized in countless movie scenes where characters decide to answer their phones or respond to text messages in the middle of discussions, music concerts – and even sex. As a nod to politeness, they might say, "Sorry, I have to take this."

Ah, how things have changed. Even as little as twenty years ago, not giving someone your undivided attention meant, at most, drumming your fingers impatiently on the table, or perhaps glancing pointedly at your watch.

It was considered polite – indeed, almost a virtue – to be fully present. It was implicit that the time spent together would not be shared with others. Imagine a person in the middle of a conversation with you suddenly getting up and saying, "Sorry, I've just remembered something!", leaving the room and coming back a few minutes later to resume the conversation. Or imagine you're in a restaurant enjoying a cosy dinner when a stranger walks up to your date and starts chatting to them for minutes on end, leaving you high and dry as you watch your food go cold.

Both scenarios would be unthinkable. Yet, if the very same interruptions are occasioned by a smartphone, it is somehow okay. Technology has effectively driven a wedge between our need to be connected and the attention we are willing to give to others.

I don't think people are being intentionally rude or disrespectful. Indeed, they may not even be aware of the effect interruptions have on others. It's just that social norms have evolved with the smartphone, and most people have adjusted to this new, connected society.

As far as possible, whether in a business or a social setting, I never have my phone visible on the table. It's out of sight. If it does ring, then I'll usually ignore it. I can't be interrupted by message notifications because they're all turned off anyway. I can always check my phone afterwards. In my social circle, I've noticed that it's those people from the pre-internet era who are most likely to adopt this relaxed attitude.

Of course, the extent to which this is possible depends on the kind of work you do, the expectations of your friends and co-workers, and your personality type. But it's also a generational thing – a mindset, really.

Those of us who lived before the age of smartphones know from personal experience that life is possible without them. We recall a time when entrepreneurs built great businesses, families maintained loving relationships, and the Apollo astronauts went successfully to the moon and back – all without the need to be interrupted every few minutes.

Chapter 15

There were advantages to being unconnected

If there's one term that perfectly captures life today, it's the state of being connected. Preferably all the time. However, before the age of the internet, this would have made no sense.

How could a person be connected? To what? To whom? Only objects or machines could be connected, not people.

Using the modern-day meaning of the term, we could say that before the internet, people were always unconnected. Unless a person was at work, in an airplane at 30,000 feet, or at some known location, they were "out" somewhere.

Being out meant you had your own space and were free to do as you wished. The notion was built into everyday life. You could read a book, go for a walk or simply do nothing. You knew that you were unreachable, and therefore uninterruptible.

Whether we call it recharging our batteries, reconnecting with ourselves or just daydreaming, we all need downtime. But in today's world, this is next to impossible, as we are constantly tethered to our smartphones and computers.

Young teens, studies show, spend up to five hours or more each day on social media, putting their private lives on display for public consumption in the relentless pursuit of peer approval.

It's not much different for adults, whose friendships and personal relationships are virtually governed by constant connectivity. You've probably seen countless movie scenes in which a character decides to switch their phone off for a few hours to enjoy some downtime. But when they switch on again, they are greeted by a deluge of text messages, emails and missed calls. You can run, but you can't hide.

Before the internet, you interacted with others face-to-face, or on the landline phone in their home or office. Outside of that, you had no way of knowing where they were or what they were doing. (As an aside, it makes you wonder whether it was easier to cheat on your partner back then because there were no cell phones, or whether it is easier today because there are. The definitive study on this has yet to be written.)

Being unconnected meant there was no external audience needing a running commentary on how your day was going. No one was required to call you or voice approval in any way. You couldn't feel envy or think about how uninteresting your own life might be. And even if your life was going amazingly well, nobody would ever know unless you specifically told them.

Constant connectivity between people has never corresponded to any vital need in society. If this really had been the case, it would have threatened the very foundation of personal and family relationships over the past few centuries. Constant connectivity between people is no more a need today than it was in 1975 or 1875. Rather, it is the *availability* of instant connectivity that has transformed it into a need – actively encouraged by social media. It's a classic illustration of the economic principle that supply creates its own demand.

There was a time not so long ago when young high-school graduates would go travelling to distant countries for up to a year – a rite-of-passage prior to starting university still known today as the gap-year. These boys and girls would keep in touch with friends and family only every couple of weeks, mainly via letter or a hastily scrawled postcard, because phone calls were expensive. Parents didn't sit at home chewing their nails in angst and worrying about their kids. Today, not hearing from them after a few weeks would probably be grounds for contacting the police and the embassy in that country, and reporting them as missing.

Unless you had probable cause for alarm – like catching a TV news report on a natural disaster or a coup d'état – you simply got on with your life and thought fondly about the good time they must be having thousands of miles away. Being unconnected was the norm, so expectations were different.

Chapter 16

Phone conversations were private

Talking on the phone during the pre-internet era was a private and confidential activity. You generally spoke quietly, and it was unusual for strangers to overhear what you were saying. Indeed, it would almost have been embarrassing.

At home, family members might have overheard you talking because the phone was invariably in the kitchen or the living room; but at least you weren't among strangers. Public phones were located in so-called silent spaces to protect the privacy of the caller and keep outside noise from drowning out your call. Street payphones were enclosed in booths which had their own door. Payphones in airports and railway stations were affixed to the wall and surrounded by a soundproof shroud. In open-plan offices, cubicles had padded, soundproof partitions.

A phone conversation was no different from any other conversation and was worthy of privacy. The fact that it took place through a piece of technology that you held to your ear did not change this basic rule of etiquette.

Today, in our connected world in which virtually everyone carries a cell phone, we live in a more socially relaxed – some might say disrespectful – age.

People use their phones in public without even lowering their voices, as if they were alone. Many don't even bother using an earpiece; and when they do, it is more for their own convenience (so they can have their hands free) than as a courtesy to others. Meanwhile, those of us in earshot have to listen to the boring details of office politics, business deals, family disputes – and even lovers' tiffs.

Far from being a fringe activity, this has practically become the norm. There are now signs in many public places –

particularly waiting rooms – exhorting people to avoid using their phones as a courtesy to others. On some trains, there are even so-called Quiet Carriages where you're not supposed to use your phone at all.

I often had to deal with such behaviour during my many years of international corporate travel. The most notorious offenders were business travellers, many of them travelling in business or first class. They'd have no compunction about turning an airport lounge or train carriage into an extension of their office. I would regularly intervene, asking them politely to hang up or go and talk somewhere else. Sometimes things got heated, but they would eventually grudgingly comply (probably less through admission of guilt than to avoid a scene).

I don't think people are deliberately being disrespectful by talking loudly in public and being oblivious to those around them. They're probably just going with the flow in the context of the times. After all, nearly everyone is doing it, so what's the problem?

If you're generally well-mannered and considerate of others in social settings, you will probably be well-mannered and considerate on your cell phone, too. You'll speak softly, and perhaps end the call quickly. Unfortunately, such old-fashioned values of politeness and decorum have declined over the past few decades.

National culture also comes into play. Anyone who has travelled a lot will know that in some cultures, people talk more loudly than others – think Americans or southern Europeans. Other cultures are the opposite, for example Japanese and northern Europeans. For example, when was the last time you found yourself having to listen to a Japanese or a Scandinavian talking loudly on their phone?

Thank heavens the use of cell phones on planes is still essentially restricted to Wi-Fi messaging. It's an implicit recognition of the fact that phone calls in the confined space of an airline cabin would be an intolerable nuisance to other passengers. If you think that road-rage is a problem, just try and imagine air-rage at 30,000 feet over the Atlantic.

Chapter 17

We wrote letters

Today, we casually dash off an email or text message in a matter of seconds, hit Send and get a reply a few minutes later. It feels almost impersonal. Indeed, the sheer speed and ease with which it happens almost detracts from its value.

Before the internet, you kept in touch by writing letters. The process took weeks rather than minutes. Indeed, the very slowness of it all made letters very personal – and also very valuable, because they couldn't just be deleted.

It was more like a ritual. You took the time to write a letter, you went to the Post Office to drop it in the letterbox, and you finally experienced the joy of receiving a reply a week or two later. It was one of life's little pleasures. People today who've only ever known the immediacy of email and social media must find it difficult to even imagine.

This very subject was explored in a family comedy I saw on television. It's about a woman who's had enough of her smartphone-addicted husband and their two adolescent children and decides to disconnect the whole household. When the teenage daughter ends up losing her boyfriend because she's no longer present on social media, she tries to win him back by writing him a letter! The novelty of the experience for him, and the intimacy he discovers in reading her handwriting, brings them back together again.

Except for business or admin letters, which were written on plain white paper and sent in plain white envelopes with ordinary stamps, letter-writing was a very personal activity. When you wrote to friends and family, you invariably put some effort into it. If you wrote to a sweetheart, you might even choose a special kind of paper in delicate shades of blue or pink, sometimes embossed with flowers or other symbols. It would convey a particular mood or tone. Love letters, not surprisingly, were often adorned with hand-drawn hearts and kisses at the bottom – essentially hand-drawn emojis.

You also ensured you had a decent pen that brought out the best of your handwriting and enhanced the message you were trying to convey. Good penmanship was important. Pages of hastily scribbled writing with a cheap ballpoint pen could unintentionally send the wrong signal.

Once a letter was ready to be posted, you might even go out of your way to buy colourful collector stamps to put on the envelope, and maybe also add a couple of stickers. It wasn't just time that went into a letter, but also money in the form of paper, pen, ink and stamps.

When you received a letter, a simple glance at the writing on the envelope was sometimes enough to let you know who it was from. I still remember each of my parents' distinctive handwriting, and the feelings they evoked. I also remember vividly the handwriting of the love letters I used to receive in my teens, and the emotional excitement they triggered. Today, I would have difficulty identifying the handwriting of my own children because our communication has always been digital.

Popular music was full of songs about people writing letters to each other – love letters, break-up letters, make-up letters and come-back letters. Some favourites when I was growing up were *The letter* in 1967, sung by the Box Tops; *Take a letter, Maria* in 1969, sung by R.B. Greaves; and *Please, Mr Postman* in 1975, sung by The Carpenters.

Many young people also had international pen-pals, which was an ideal way to learn more about other cultures and countries. Such relationships between people who'd never met were based entirely on the exchange of letters.

Quite clearly then, writing letters wasn't just some functional activity in which you hastily scribbled a few paragraphs onto a page. You went the extra mile. A really chatty letter could run to several pages and even reach a thousand words. That's an entire evening gone right there. It wasn't uncommon to tell a friend you couldn't go out with them because you had to stay in to write a letter. It was almost like laundry night.

Unlike today's digital communication, which is either deleted or quickly forgotten, letters weren't just thrown away. The really personal ones were often kept for many years – sometimes decades – perhaps wrapped in blue or pink ribbon and lovingly kept in a box on a shelf somewhere. My parents kept all the long letters my brother and I wrote home to them during our years at university in France. We still read them today whenever we want to relive those times. Such was the value of handwritten communication.

Chapter 18

People could disagree and still be polite to each other

I disapprove of what you say, but I will defend to the death your right to say it. This well-known saying is attributed to the French enlightenment writer and philosopher, Voltaire, and is often described as the very foundation of freedom of speech.

Today's modern-day equivalent in the divisive age of social media would probably sound more like this: Not only do I disapprove of what you say, but you're a ["INSERT PREFERRED EXPLETIVE"] and your views are not welcome here!

The internet is a great democratizer. It provides a platform to anyone to offer an opinion on anything, at any time, to millions of people – and it's completely unfiltered and free of censorship. But this ultimate freedom comes with a downside. Combined with the steady erosion of old-fashioned values of decorum and respect over the past few decades, it has made it easy to vilify those we don't agree with – and even get enthusiastic support for doing so.

Even as little as twenty years ago, it would have been inconceivable to crudely insult somebody you disagreed with in an open forum without being publicly shamed or asked to leave. Today, it can get you a thousand likes, more subscribers to your YouTube channel and perhaps even an invitation to a talk show.

The sheer volume of information online, combined with the propensity for extreme points of view, have resulted in the polarization of debate. This is particularly notable in areas such as politics, race and gender. It's almost as if there is no longer any middle ground, even for those who wish to position themselves there. Extremism and outrage, often expressed under the cloak of anonymity, seem to have neutralized any rational discussion.

To be sure, people were intolerant of others' views long before the age of email, blogs and social media. But the internet has provided an easy technological platform to globally amplify intolerance and garner support from around the world.

Before the internet, people spoke to each other in public in forums like lecture halls, auditoriums, and radio or TV studios. Since only one person could speak at a time, such forums were necessarily highly structured, with a host moderating the discussion. And because you could fit only so many people into a closed space, the audience was necessarily limited in size.

Apart perhaps from radio phone-in programmes, there were no public forums in which large groups of people had simultaneous access to each other's views, as is the case with social media today. This was not technologically possible in a paper-based society. The most you could do was write a letter to a newspaper or magazine, but you couldn't exchange views with other readers – at least not unless the editor decided to publish a reply from someone else a week later. By then, it might not have mattered that much to you any longer.

In these limited public forums, people would adhere to the social norms of the times in terms of formality, courtesy and etiquette, no matter how much they might disagree with each other. The moderator would quickly step in to pull violators back into line. An impolite or extremely negative letter to a newspaper or magazine would be edited for tone – or simply not published if it went too far.

You were just never rude or impolite to those you disagreed with. This etiquette was part of the social, cultural and media landscape. You only have to watch interviews, lectures and debates of the pre-internet era to see this. Sometimes, it was a respect that bordered on prudery.

I still remember back in 1979 when United States president Jimmy Carter made a somewhat shocking statement – at least by the standards of the time. Speaking to a group of Congressmen at a White House dinner, Carter said that if Senator Kennedy dared to challenge him for the Democratic Nomination the following year, "I'll whip his ass!"

The word "ass" would barely raise an eyebrow today. But television and newspapers were very circumspect in how they reported it, preferring to use innuendo or euphemism (e.g., posterior). An article in *Time* entitled "Press: Whip His What?", explains how one newspaper in Los Angeles used three dots, leaving the rest to the imagination, and another ran a headline that read coyly: *Carter Flexes his Whip Arm.*

It was a more innocent time. Media power was concentrated in the hands of major newspapers and television channels. Old-fashioned standards of civility prevailed. But in today's era of blogs, YouTube and social media, we have all become our own newspapers and television channels. Unfortunately, this heady power to comment on the issues of the day has not always been matched by a willingness to be respectful of opposing viewpoints.

Chapter 19

Relationships required socialization

Today you can start, maintain and even end a relationship on your laptop or smartphone. Before the internet, however, making friends and dating required human contact and face-to-face communication. You had to leave the house, meet people and talk to them.

The only real technology at your disposal was your landline telephone, but that wasn't going to get you very far. Calls were expensive and not always private, especially if you lived at home where family members could listen in on your conversations.

Of course, you could also write a letter to the person you were interested in, but it might take a week or more before you got a reply. Far easier to just go out, meet people face to face and rely on your looks and sparkling personality. If you wanted to go out on a date, you had to pluck up the courage and ask. There was no technology to hide behind. You had to perform in public and make yourself vulnerable. It was a tough time for the shy and the introverted. This was a staple in pre-internet sitcoms, which invariably had some angst-ridden or socially inept main character who just couldn't land a date.

Parties, movies, hanging out together in malls or coffee shops – a social life back then was very active. It wasn't something virtual conducted from the comfort of an armchair. You went out. You spent money on coffee, drinks and movie tickets.

The people you met were their real selves, warts and all, not an artificial, curated online profile. Their qualities and imperfections couldn't be airbrushed or photoshopped away. What you saw was what you got.

This real-world socialization had the advantage of facilitating spontaneous meetings between people of different social, educational and ethnic backgrounds. Such matches are less probable on social media and dating apps, which tend to steer people towards similar rather than dissimilar profiles.

Seeing others in a real social setting also allowed you to appreciate a whole range of other qualities such as their conversational skills, empathy or sense of humour. These are essential in any potential relationship, but are harder to pick up in dating apps and social media, where the focus is on looks.

Social media and dating apps have, of course, dramatically expanded the available pool of friends and partners. It's an almost perfect marketplace. It not only matches supply with demand, but focuses on people who are actually looking for partners. But like all marketplaces, it comes at the expense of a certain commoditization, to use an economic term. People become mere commodities whose market value – especially that of women – is primarily dependent on their looks.

Social media also comes with its own set of challenges. The most fundamental one is the time, effort and stress involved in creating and maintaining an online profile. This is especially problematic for teens, who practically can't exist socially in their peer group without one. As any teen will tell you (in private), this is a high-maintenance and stressful activity. For example, taking a selfie or replying to a text message shouldn't take more than a minute. In reality, it can easily take half an hour as people agonize over just the right pose or choice of words that would show how "nonchalantly cool" they are. And then you've got to be constantly monitoring your messages so that you can be part of the conversation. It never ends!

Dating apps bring an additional challenge. After getting over that first hurdle of creating an attractive dating profile – sometimes with professional assistance – you then have to get through that crucial first meeting when both parties have to drop the mask. There will usually be a gap – sometimes a significant one – between the actual person and the carefully projected self who was chatting online behind the safety of a screen. It's a high-pressure situation as each party weighs up the probability of there being a second meeting.

How much simpler it all was before the internet, when there was no profile to maintain – except, perhaps, that of your body. You took reasonable care of your looks and you dressed with a minimum of fashion sense. Then you went out, met people and hoped for the best. You win some, you lose some. C'est la vie.

Chapter 20

People spoke to each other in restaurants

I was having lunch in a restaurant the other day when I saw a sight that has, alas, become all too familiar – a party of diners cut off from each other and not talking much because they were mostly hooked up to their mobile technology.

It was a family of four sitting just across the table from me – husband, wife, teenage son, and daughter aged about eight. The husband was on his phone, dealing with a business call (I was close enough to hear the conversation, and he was talking loudly enough for me to hear). The wife was staring vacantly around her, waiting for him to finish. The teenage son was busy texting, with a mischievous smile on his face. His sister was happily playing on her fold-out iPad, which Mom had carefully set up for her moments earlier.

Just before the husband finished his call, the wife's phone rang. She answered. The roles were now reversed, and he waited for her to finish. I stopped watching this comedy when my waiter stepped into view and placed my seafood dish in front of me. While enjoying my meal, I stole occasional glances at the family opposite. Not much had changed. There was still very little conversation, and the meal was mostly a lot of phoning and texting, interrupted by the need to swallow food. Though the family was together, it wasn't exactly quality time.

In all fairness, other diners were talking animatedly to each other, and the restaurant did have a nice lunchtime vibe. But equally, I couldn't help noticing how often conversation would come to a stop at various tables because someone needed to answer their phone or make an urgent call. I eat out often enough for my observations of other diners and their cell-phone behaviour to constitute a social experiment in itself, especially as my own phone is out of sight. Here are some patterns I've noticed.

Firstly, phones are always placed directly onto the table, either next to the side plate or right in the middle of the table. There's no mistaking what that means: other people are as important as those sitting at the table.

Secondly, even a romantic tête-à-tête can be subject to interruptions. Typically, one person will answer the phone with a token apology while the other waits. And waits. And if conversation should suddenly dry up, one of them, or sometimes both simultaneously, will reach for their phones and start scrolling and checking for messages. This type of behaviour is somehow just expected; indeed, technology has succeeded in legitimizing it.

I recall a cartoon many years ago in which a man and his date are in a cosy restaurant enjoying a candlelit dinner. She is rather quiet and just sits there. He remarks, with obvious concern, "Are you okay? You haven't touched your phone all evening."

This kind of thing never happened before the internet. Phones hadn't yet arrived to give people a free pass to tune out of the conversation. The only interruptions were the waiter stopping at your table to take your order, bring your food and occasionally see if you wanted anything else. Of course, if you really wanted a timeout, you could always go to the bathroom. But otherwise, it was just you and the person you were dining with. You had to talk to each other. If an awkward silence developed, well, you stared pointedly at your plate and hoped it wouldn't last too long. The notion of going out to a restaurant together, and then spending most of the time communicating to people who were not even physically present, would have been unthinkable.

You had to be really influential to enjoy the luxury of being disturbed by a phone call, for the simple reason that the phone was a fixed-line device that belonged to the restaurant. A common scene in movies from the pre-internet era was that of a waiter hovering into view and whispering solicitously into the ear of the very important man (it was usually a man) that there was a phone call for him. He would then offer profuse apologies for the unseemly interruption, leave the table and then disappear to answer the phone.

In short, before the era of constant connectivity, going to eat out in a restaurant with someone was usually a special occasion. It often required making a reservation, dressing up and enjoying a couple of hours of company and conversation. Going to all that trouble just to sit there and not talk to each other would have made no sense. You might as well have stayed at home.

LEISURE

Chapter 21

Reading books was part of everyday life

Quick – look around you. What is everyone doing? If you're in a public place like a train, restaurant or waiting room, the chances are that most of them are staring at their smartphones.

Few will be reading a book, newspaper or magazine. Fewer still will be lost in their thoughts doing nothing. In the days before the internet, nearly all of these people would have been reading.

Reading books – particularly novels – was one of the main forms of leisure. It was so ingrained in your upbringing and education that you usually had a novel with you to while away the time in the bus, the train or the doctor's waiting room. On a rainy day, you happily curled up in bed with a good book.

If you were going on a long flight, then you definitely took a novel with you, especially as inflight entertainment wasn't as developed as it is today. In fact, "airport novel" is the term used even today to describe this kind of literature, which is typically fast-paced, entertaining and undemanding. They're still sold in bookshops in the departure lounges of major airports. In France, the equivalent is *roman de gare* (railway-station novel), harking back to the days when travellers needed to keep themselves busy on long train journeys. Kiosks in railway stations all over the world still sell them.

If you didn't buy your book at a bookstore, you borrowed it free of charge from the public library. My brother and I grew up hanging about in public libraries, mainly because that's where our mother used to stock up on her reading material. Amazon and the age of online books was still many years away, so traditional book publishing was big business. High-street bookstores were large and stocked a huge selection of books, from easy-to-read fiction to heavily intellectual non-fiction. You could spend hours browsing the shelves.

Whenever my brother came to visit me when I was still living in Paris, he would always take a day out of his holiday for book-buying. He would get onto the Eurostar train and do a day trip to London's bustling Oxford Street, where there was a big concentration of mega-bookstores like Borders, Foyles and Waterstones. On his return later in the evening, his shopping bag would be heaving with books.

At home, your bookshelf reflected your tastes. Unlike books on your phone, tablet or e-reader, which only you can see, physical books are visible to others. They therefore served to advertise your tastes in reading, from historic novels and romance to mysteries and thrillers. Questions like, "Can I see what you're reading?" or "Can I check out your bookshelf?" were commonplace among friends and family.

Books even lent themselves to pick-up lines. If the good-looking stranger sitting across from you in the train was reading something with the cover clearly visible, you could say something like, "Hi. Is this his latest? I haven't got around to it yet. Would you recommend it?" Connecting like this with a potential dating partner gave both parties an immediate insight into the other's personality, conversational skills and sense of humour. It beats a swipe-right any day!

Today, you might make a social statement with your model of smartphone, tablet or laptop. Back then, you made it with the book you were reading. It revealed not just your literary tastes, but also your personality type. An Agatha Christie mystery said one thing about you, a Barbara Cartland romance quite another. Then there were the intricately plotted stories from the likes of Irwin Shaw, John Fowles and Leon Uris. These blockbusters, which delved into serious subjects like science, history and politics, typically ran to over five hundred pages and marked you out as a bit of an intellectual.

Of course, print books today are far from dead. They still hold their own in the global marketplace, despite the Amazon revolution and the presence of cheap eBooks across multiple online platforms. Surveys in many countries show that readers prefer print books over eBooks. They're just easier to hold and page through; they are also unbreakable and have infinite battery life.

I read many books on my Kindle, especially when I discover something new that I want to read right away. However, I still prefer a print book. I like its artistic design, the way it sits in my hand, and the feel of my fingers on the page. A print book also has a familiar, comforting smell that an e-reader could never have – though I certainly wouldn't put it past the designers to incorporate a palette of artificial smells in future models.

Chapter 22

We knew how to read maps

Before the arrival of satellite navigation in cars and phones, the only way you could find your way around – short of asking for directions – was to consult a map. They came in various formats.

There were folding maps, which were usually kept in the glove compartment of your car. They opened up into a single sheet of paper, and then folded back into place – except when wrongly done. This might prompt an angry outburst like, "Who the hell folded this map?!"

Then there were the more practical maps in booklet format. They could easily fit into a handbag or pocket, and were useful for finding your way around town, especially when you were visiting a foreign country.

Finally, there were large maps at the exits of railway stations that showed the major streets, shops and landmarks. They were typically affixed to the wall, just as you were about to head out.

Unlike Google Maps and their equivalents today, which are entirely passive, the maps of that era required some brainwork on the part of the user. You didn't just hear a voice telling you to turn left at the next intersection. You had to develop spatial awareness – in other words, you needed a picture in your head of where you were and where you were heading. You then used a system of vertical and horizontal coordinates to pinpoint the exact location of your destination.

For example, if you were visiting Lisbon and trying to locate the Torre de Belém in your tourist map booklet, you would turn to the index at the back, alphabetically arranged for ease of reference. You would then read, for example: *Torre de Belém, 45 – D3*. Translation: turn to the map on page 45. Run your finger up the side until you locate D, then across until you locate 3. The intersection of these two coordinates would give you the precise location.

Map-reading was an essential part of everyday life, and you might easily get lost or turn up late for a meeting without this basic skill. In an age where gender stereotypes were rife, women were often playfully mocked for having less spatial ability than men. This was reflected in a humorous best-seller at the time entitled *Why Men Don't Listen and Women Can't Read Maps*, by Barbara and Allan Pease.

The most popular city-centre map booklets were perennial best-sellers, selling countless millions of copies, particularly in big cities like London and Paris. Virtually everybody had one safely tucked away in their back pocket or their handbag. If you were driving, you often had it open on the passenger seat so that you could quickly consult it at a red light.

Today, if you're lost in a new city or need to get from A to B, there's no shortage of navigational apps on your phone or in your car to help you. You don't even need to orient yourself or know which route you're taking; you just have to follow instructions. This passive navigation doesn't necessarily lead to the development of spatial reasoning, or the ability to visualize where places are in relation to each other.

There have been countless amusing newspaper articles about drivers getting hopelessly lost with their satellite navigation and ending up in the weirdest of places – including a lake, a cliff edge and even another country. Little wonder that many digital natives no longer feel confident about using maps and have difficulty getting around without the help of satellite navigation.

Many of us who grew up with maps find it hard to just blindly follow the instructions of a satellite-navigation system. For example, when I'm driving to an unknown street address,

I sometimes go online first and look at my itinerary on Google Maps. This helps me to orient myself spatially and familiarize myself with key landmarks. That way, I can make more sense of the GPS instructions once I'm on the road. Otherwise, I feel I'm just navigating blind and could end up anywhere – perhaps even in a lake.

Chapter 23

Travel had the power to surprise

Think of a tourist destination you haven't been to yet – perhaps Sydney, Los Angeles or the South of France. The good news is you don't have to wait to discover it; you can go there right now by watching tourist videos online.

Perhaps you already have.

Google "walking tour of Sydney", and you'll find yourself experiencing the shops, monuments and streets of Australia's most populous city. You can even check out the rooms of various hotels and see if you like the views of the harbour.

How about a pleasant drive between Cannes and Nice on the winding Mediterranean coastal road? Google "driving Cannes to Nice" and the videos are there, shot in high definition and putting you in the driver's seat.

How about experiencing the onboard service of the airline you'll be flying on? Well, you can check that out, too. YouTube is chock-full of aviation bloggers who film their full inflight experience, from the food and wine to the inflight movies and even the bathrooms.

It won't be long before 3D headsets enable you to experience all of this in mind-bending virtual reality. Which does rather beg the question: why even bother going there at all? After all, your trip will largely consist of confirming what you've already seen on-screen, with just the added dimension of the real smells and sounds.

Before the internet, this ability to visit other places from the comfort of your desk or armchair was impossible. Of course, there were photographs in magazines and travel brochures, and perhaps the odd TV travel programme. But these were nothing compared to the real thing.

Back then, going on vacation in a foreign country was a major exercise that required elaborate planning and preparation. You had to go to a travel agency, page through travel brochures, and explore flight and destination options. You had to go to your local bank and order travellers' cheques, because international credit cards were not yet widely accepted, and you couldn't withdraw cash from foreign ATMs.

Then came the big day when you went to the airport, which was an event in itself. Right through to the 1980s, flying was still a novelty. You dressed up for the occasion, and didn't just turn up in jeans and sneakers. Friends and family would come to the airport to see you off. You'd then clear customs and go directly to the boarding gates, as there was no pesky airport security in those days. You could even board with a Swiss Army knife, which was usually a standard part of the average traveller's hand-luggage.

Not long after take-off, you'd hear this inflight announcement: "The seatbelt signs have been switched off. Passengers may now smoke." Yes, you were still allowed to light up in the air, albeit in the smoking section. You then settled down to your inflight entertainment, which usually consisted of reading the inflight magazine, a newspaper or a book.

On long-haul flights, you could watch the inflight movie on a big screen positioned in the centre section of each cabin. Individual seatback screens didn't appear until the late 1980s. Indeed, until the advent of low-cost airlines and the democratization of air travel in the 1990s, it was often said that the flight itself was the entertainment.

You finally arrived at your destination and checked into your hotel. Next morning, after having cashed some of your travellers' cheques for local currency, you strapped on your most comfortable shoes, applied your suntan lotion and walked the streets. Monuments, beaches, museums, restaurants – your visit would be a total visual, auditory and olfactory rush, made even more memorable by the sheer novelty of it all.

I still remember the first time I touched down on European soil. It was at Nice Airport in France in 1980, during a brief stopover on my way to Paris for my university studies. It was like stepping into a new dimension. Everything felt novel: the biting cold temperature outside at six o'clock in the morning; the sounds of French being spoken everywhere; and the constant bumping into other people because they gave way to the right and not to the left. But perhaps the biggest surprise of all, after a lifetime of living in Africa, was the sight of white women cleaning the airport toilets!

As my brother vividly recalls in his book, *The Scholarship Kids*, where he describes our arrival in Nice: "Our stereotypes were coming under severe pressure. Like Dorothy in *The Wizard of Oz*, we had entered a topsy-turvy world where up was down, left was right, and black was white. We sure weren't in Kansas anymore." (Robert Gentle, 2023)

Of course, the power of travel to surprise can cut both ways. Sometimes, there were unpleasant surprises – a hotel room overlooking a busy street, a favourite landmark closed off for renovations, or a much-touted restaurant turning out to be a total disappointment. But despite this, your general impression would usually be one of pleasant discovery, because novelty is often its own surprise.

Today, novelty is no longer possible because of the deluge of tourist information on the internet, from photos and videos to livestream webcams. Once you get to your destination, perhaps the only real surprise is that the excessively upbeat material you viewed on the internet doesn't really correspond to reality. It's one reason that travellers prompted for reviews are invariably asked the question, "How well did the photos describe your actual experience?"

Perversely, this question seems to argue for the premise that the ideal holiday should contain no surprises. Is that even desirable? We have essentially lost the sense of freedom and adventure of being unconnected, and the surprise of discovering new people and places. We've already previewed it all online before even stepping onto the plane. It might still be a great holiday – only a much more predictable one.

Chapter 24

Movie plots were more creative

The internet has sucked out much of the creativity from modern movies – at least that's what it feels like to those of us from the pre-internet era. They rely far too heavily on technology, instead of good old-fashioned storytelling, to move the plot along.

We notice this in scenes of everyday life that form part of the story. Typical examples are people being late, having to follow someone, trying to locate a person and – usually the most common – getting an urgent message to someone.

People are instantly reachable; their phone gives their exact location; they can track a person's movements based on where they last used a credit card; they can take a picture and instantly send it to someone; they can copy confidential information onto a USB flash disk; they can surreptitiously record a conversation without having to wear a wire; they can retrace a person's movements by checking the previous destinations in a car's GPS navigation system; they can watch CCTV footage to see what actually happened. And so on and so forth.

All of these scenes, and much more, are part and parcel of any movie that takes place in the internet age. Some scriptwriters, however, shy away from the hi-tech approach and try and limit the role of smartphones and the internet where possible. For example, when they want someone to be genuinely lost or stranded, they fall back on the most obvious tricks, like a person forgetting their phone at home, being low on battery, or being in an area without cell-phone coverage.

Back in the 20th century, however, scenes like following someone, finding a person or sending an urgent message, were played out very differently. The only technologies moving the plot along were cars, fixed-line phones and analogue cameras. The rest was achieved through people uncovering information and discovering facts through movement, observation and improvisation. Or through the simple actions of everyday life. For example, you might be late for a rendezvous because your watch had stopped. Or you couldn't find a payphone to warn someone of danger. Or you had to go knocking on doors and show people a photo to find a missing person.

Unhampered by the amazing technological progress of mobile communications and the internet, scriptwriters and authors therefore had a wealth of options when it came to creative scenarios and plots.

For example, a payphone – perhaps on a street corner or in a restaurant – was often a useful plot device because several people invariably wanted to use it quite urgently. So, you had the opportunity to build interesting scenarios around people waiting in line, arguing about who goes first, or experiencing a setback when there is no answer. If such scenes had to be rewritten today in an age of cell phones, it would require a complete rethink. Sometimes, not even a rethink will do. Many classic movies from the pre-internet era – for example, *Home Alone* and *The Parent Trap* – would not even be possible today because the essential premise on which they are based (the inability to communicate with someone on the other side of the world) has been rendered obsolete by technology.

Or consider that staple of action thrillers, the hostage movie, in which a building is seized by bank robbers or terrorists who take the occupants hostage. With the phone lines cut, no one can raise the alarm. But if everyone had had smartphones, they could have notified the authorities immediately – with video footage into the bargain – and the movie would have been over before it even started.

So next time you're watching a modern film characterized by excessive use of smartphones, laptops and Google, ask yourself whether it might not have been a better idea for the scriptwriters to dial down the technology and get back to storytelling basics. In fact, this is a question that the producers of the 2022 hit movie *Top Gun: Maverick* must surely have asked themselves. It would explain why the story was built around outmoded dogfights and an old-fashioned, low-level bombing run that put the pilots at great risk of being shot down. I found this premise totally implausible in today's age of ultra-sophisticated guided weaponry, but it made for a far more thrilling movie.

Of course, movies will always reflect the dominant technology of their era; it cannot be otherwise. But when the technology is overdone, it can make for less creative plots.

WORK

Chapter 25

There was no email distraction

These days, you take a break from your email correspondence if you want to get some work done. Before the internet, you took a break from your work if you wanted to get some correspondence done.

To understand this seemingly bizarre statement, you need to consider the technology of business correspondence back then.

Before desktop computers, Microsoft Word and email, correspondence in the workplace was done by letter. You usually dictated it to your secretary, who knew how to take notes in shorthand, an extremely rapid form of writing that uses symbols and abbreviations instead of whole words. She (secretaries were almost always women) would then type your letter on a typewriter. Asking a secretary to "take a letter" was so ingrained in the language of the day that it even became the title of a 1969 hit song by American soul singer R.B. Greaves, entitled *Take a letter, Maria*.

Because you typed straight onto paper, you had to get it right the first time. If you made a typo, you couldn't just hit Backspace, delete it and fix it. Instead, you applied a white correcting fluid onto the wrong word, just like you'd apply nail polish to your nails – with a little brush attached to the cap of the bottle. You waited for it to dry, and then typed the word again – correctly this time. The most popular brand of correcting fluid was Tipp-Ex. It even became a verb – to *tippex* or *tippex out* a typo. Tipp-Ex was to offices what Tabasco sauce is to restaurants – there was a bottle on every typist's desk.

But the time and effort required in writing a letter did have one big advantage: you would rarely receive more than a handful at any given time. Letters were reserved for official communications, especially with customers, suppliers and other organizations. After all, you wouldn't write a letter to your colleague a few offices away from you. You'd pick up the phone, or simply walk over and talk to them.

After the arrival of email, however, people soon realized that it was much easier to just fire off a hasty message with a few lines rather than to gather one's thoughts and actually talk to someone (not to mention having to deal with the obligatory social niceties of office life). So, they soon stopped using the telephone in favour of email. People are therefore inundated with the stuff and receive up to a hundred or more each day. They seem to spend more time battling this avalanche of correspondence than doing the work they were hired for.

I lived through the entire transition from letters to email, and what a ride it was. In my first job in IT in the early 1980s, there was no email. There were no laptops or cell phones either. On my frequent international flights, I had the time to think and come up with new ideas. For relaxation, I read my novel. During my rides to the hotel or the airport, I talked to the taxi driver. What a simple, pleasant time.

It didn't last. The cell phone, the laptop and the internet were starting to change the workplace. Slowly but surely, I became reachable. In the 1990s, I found myself having to use dial-up technology in hotels to connect to the company network, which then gave me secure access to the internet. By the early 2000s, the beast had been fully unleashed and there was no longer anywhere to hide. Talking to taxi drivers became a thing of the past. I was now using the time to check my email and make calls on my Blackberry.

Email now interrupts us everywhere. Before the Covid pandemic made remote working a way of life, one of the biggest challenges of the workplace was whether you should be checking your email at home. Yet this has never been part of any HR policy, nor does it figure in anyone's job description or work contract. Indeed, unless it is explicitly required, it is illegal. And yet, it slowly became the norm, as people reckoned it was good for their careers to stay connected outside of office hours.

Today, something of a backlash against email has developed. As far back as 2011, German companies like Volkswagen and Deutsche Telekom, as well as various German government departments, introduced new rules preventing workers from being systematically contacted at home or on vacation. In 2017, France passed a "right-to-disconnect" law that requires employers to establish blackout hours for email. In 2021, the Victoria Police in Australia won the right to disconnect outside of working hours, except in emergencies.

But for far too many workers around the world, unfortunately, email continues to be an electronic scourge from which there seems to be no escape, whether they're at their desks, on the road or at home.

Chapter 26

You couldn't take work home with you

Perhaps it's time to update all those warm, fuzzy sayings about home. *Home is where the heart is.* Maybe, but it's also where the laptop is. *A man's home is his castle.* Not anymore. The castle walls have been breached, and a person's home is now also their office.

Even before Covid, home was already no longer the place where we switched off after work. If anything, it was where we switched on again, thanks to the all-pervasive presence of the internet. Home Hi-Fi gave way to home Wi-Fi, and the dance of work continued late into the evening, sometimes long after the kids had been put to bed.

Now that hybrid working has become the norm, this scenario has intensified. For millions of people, home is now also the office, thanks to the magic – or the curse – of round-the-clock connectivity. Work-life balance has given way to work-life integration, as the two seem to blur into a seamless whole interrupted only by the need to eat, sleep and procreate.

Before the internet, work could only be done in specific locations like offices, factories or stores, because that's where all the information was – and it was on paper. Even data stored on company computers – say, customer or billing information – still needed to be printed onto paper before people could work with it. Tools such as typewriters, fax machines, photocopiers and computer terminals were also at the workplace. Products and services were therefore tightly associated with specific locations. You couldn't take stuff home with you; it was practically nailed to the floor.

The pre-internet workplace was, in a sense, one huge factory organized for the efficient production, circulation and storage of paper. It was handwritten, typed, printed and photocopied. It took the form of memos, letters, orders and invoices. Employees from the mailroom were on their feet all day, going from office to office, dropping paper off and picking paper up. A lot of it went to the Post Office as mail destined for customers and suppliers. If it was really urgent, it was sent to an overnight courier service like Federal Express (today FedEx) – hence the company's famous marketing slogan from the 1970s and 1980s: *When it absolutely, positively has to be there overnight.*

So, when you left your place of work at the end of the day, your work was over. Yay! Office hours or working hours meant just that: it was when you were at the office or at work. Of course, you might take an urgent report home to read, or grade some exam papers if you were a teacher, but these were exceptions peculiar to certain professions. Generally, once you left work, your job was effectively on hold until you returned the next day. Not for nothing is the term "nine to five" so much a part of our collective consciousness as the start and end of a typical working day.

The traditional boundary between home and work is even reflected in language. In English, for example, you used to "knock off" from work, a term that has a rather pleasant finality about it. If you're "off the clock", it's even clearer. In German, the end of the working day is known as *Feierabend*, a combination of *feier* (to celebrate) and *abend* (evening).

When you walked out of the office, store or factory at the end of the day, you disconnected from work both physically and mentally. You came home, took off your work clothes and got into home-and-family mode. You went out for drinks, visited friends, or went to a restaurant or movie. If you were a parent, you played with the kids, had dinner together as a family, and then curled up in front of the TV to watch a favourite programme. My parents were both teachers, and they always disconnected from work in the evening by reading – my mother, novels; my father, newspapers.

In today's stressed internet age, many people need to go on vacation to be able to enjoy these banal, everyday leisure activities – and even then, they run the risk of being contacted by email or text message.

Chapter 27

There were lots of secretaries in the workplace

Today, one of the first things you notice in a typical office environment is the near absence of secretaries (or administrative assistants). And when you do find them, they may be shared among a whole team or department. Even directors sometimes share secretaries.

Before the internet, however, secretaries were everywhere. And they were invariably women. They typed letters, filed documents and managed calls. They prepared meetings, took minutes and made the coffee. They purchased stationery, booked business travel and tracked expenses. In short, they kept the workplace running like a well-oiled machine.

This might be enough to make some people from today see red and shout gender discrimination at such sexist organizations. But that would be judging the past by the standards of the present.

The reality is that the workplace back then was simply reflecting – as it always does – the technological and social realities of the time. The height of technological sophistication in the average office in the 1970s was an old-style rotary telephone, a mechanical typewriter and a very basic photocopier that didn't even do colour. Even the humble fax machine would only appear a decade later.

All the tools we take for granted today that facilitate office admin – email, Google, Word, Excel, PowerPoint – didn't exist. Documents had to be written by hand, letters typed on typewriters, spreadsheets done manually with calculators, presentations prepared using plastic transparencies, and documents delivered by hand or mailed through the Post Office.

Most of this work was managed and done by secretaries, who were a major – and critical – component of the workforce. Indeed, it was only when these unsung heroes were ill or on vacation that their absence was felt. Never mind a strike by pilots or air-traffic controllers to bring the nation to a standstill; a strike by secretaries would have done it. After slowly shaking off their image as nothing more than mothers and housekeepers, women had started entering the workforce in large numbers and forging their own careers. Being a secretary was the easiest and most natural way in. It was a highly sought-after and respected profession, and was a useful pathway into a male-dominated corporate environment.

Today, with computers and smartphones, almost all secretarial duties have been offloaded to employees themselves. Before the internet, however, this was not possible. Taking over even a small part of a secretary's tasks would have left a manager with little time to do their own job.

Take phone calls. Before digital displays on office phones in the 1990s, there was no way of knowing who was calling. So, you *had* to answer. I remember that one of the greatest benefits I used to get from my secretary was the filtering of unwelcome calls, and the taking of messages when I was out of the office. I also appreciated her filing my expense reports after my frequent international travel. Of course, I could have done this myself, but given my extensive – and expensive – corporate responsibilities, would it have made economic sense for the company?

Secretaries were also very effective at organizing meetings – much more so than in today's modern workplace, with its inefficient back-and-forth emails, polling apps and shared calendars. A secretary would simply phone up each participant (or their secretary) to check availability, or just walk to their offices with her appointment planner in hand. Sometimes, simple is best.

The role of the secretary is sorely missed in today's internet age. Having one is arguably on the top of the wish-list of every manager looking for ways to reduce their administrative workload, which takes time away from their real job.

Of course, some things are far more productively done by employees themselves, particularly correspondence, reports and presentations. However, other tasks are a waste of valuable managerial time, particularly the scheduling of international meetings, the booking of business travel and the filing of expense reports. The alleged cost savings from managers doing such work themselves are no more plausible than those used to justify open-plan offices in the name of greater employee collaboration and productivity.

Companies that have run the numbers, especially smaller outfits with limited resources, have concluded that secretarial assistance can still make business sense. Some have turned to a category of secretary known as the Virtual Assistant, or VA (as opposed to the Personal Assistant, or PA). Modern internet technology allows VAs to work from home (or even in another country) for multiple clients. They handle everything from appointments and phone calls to business travel and expense reports. VAs are essentially the secretarial equivalent of outsourced call-centre agents.

The secretary or assistant still lives on, only in a different incarnation made possible by the wonders of modern communications technology.

OTHER

Chapter 28

Patience was part of everyday life

In pre-internet times, before the age of instant gratification, few things were immediately available. You had to wait for stuff to happen.

This was especially true for entertainment and leisure.

TV shows and series were aired weekly. If you didn't want to lose the plot in, say, *Columbo* or *Yes, Prime Minister*, then you'd stay in that evening. If you missed an episode, you'd have to find out from someone else what happened. In a nod to this era, streaming sites such as Netflix and HBO have adopted the same approach for certain new series.

If you didn't have the latest hit music, you waited for the weekly Top-10 hit parade on the radio or TV. If you wanted to go to a music concert, you stood in line at a store or outlet to buy your ticket. This could take up to half an hour or more, depending on who the artist was. And if you wanted a really good seat, you got up early on the day the tickets went on sale.

There were typically only three weather forecasts per day: morning, noon and night. You relied mostly on the morning one, knowing that the midday one was still hours away. Those were the days when the weather still had the power to surprise.

If you took a picture with your camera, you waited until the entire roll of film – usually 24 or 36 exposures – was used up. That could take weeks, especially if you only took pictures on special occasions like birthdays or vacations. You then dropped off your roll of film at a photo-processing lab to be developed, which would take another few days. By then, the memory of some of the photos may well have faded.

The letter from your loved one that you were eagerly waiting for might not arrive in the mail for at least another week. And so on.

These cycles, imposed by the technological limitations of the time, were as natural as the rising of the sun and the passing of the seasons. You couldn't hurry them along any more than you could make water boil faster.

Today, however, we have been conditioned by the internet to expect things to happen quickly. If you don't get an instant reply to your text message or email, your most likely reaction is that something's wrong, or that the other person doesn't want to reply. The fact that they might simply be busy doesn't even cross your mind.

Instant gratification has almost become an inalienable right, along with life, liberty and the pursuit of happiness. I want it, and I want it now! A ten-minute delay on the pizza you've just ordered feels like an hour; a thirty-second wait for a file to download feels like an eternity. Some companies promise to deliver your groceries in just fifteen minutes – as if anything longer would ruin your entire day.

The internet offers us such a wide range of products and services that we no longer take the time to really try something out. Why bother when there's another one just a click away? Our fingers swipe up in a blur, and our mouse hovers constantly on different options as we embark on a perpetual quest for the next best thing.

When you have access to almost 100 million songs on Spotify or Deezer, and around 20,000 titles on sites like Netflix and Amazon Prime, the tendency to want to flip to something new after a short while is very high. This reality is reflected in the business model of certain music-streaming sites, which only pay out royalties to artists if a song is listened to for more than thirty seconds. The days of long intros in music is over. Songwriters try to get to the chorus as quickly as possible to pass that crucial 30-second royalty threshold.

Movies get going fairly quickly, for fear that restless viewers with short attention spans might click out or flip to something else. Scriptwriters learning the craft are advised to get as quickly as possible to the inciting incident, which is defined as the event that sets the story in motion – for example, the murder in a crime drama or the boy-meets-girl moment in a romantic comedy. The story should move swiftly from scene to scene, with as few dead spots as possible. If you're a fan of classic movies from the 1970s or 1980s, you may have noticed how much more languid and slow-paced they feel compared to today's movies, with their minimal dialogue and quick cuts.

How different it all was before the internet, when we had a natural degree of patience that would seem almost virtuous to people today.

Chapter 29

Physical activity was part of everyday life

These days, you can almost run your entire life from the comfort of your armchair. You can pay your bills, check your bank statements, catch up on your correspondence and do your work. You can even order yourself a new armchair.

You're hardly likely to work up a sweat, though. Going to the kitchen to get another coffee is hardly likely to get your muscles moving. Of course, your fingers get a real workout from all that pointing, clicking and scrolling; but that's hardly going to bring your weight down.

Before the internet, the only thing you did in your armchair was relax, watch television or perhaps read a book. For everything else, you had to get up and move around. A lot.

To answer the phone at home, you had to get up and walk over to it. To buy food and groceries, you had to leave the house and go to a store. For banking operations, you went to the nearest ATM or bank branch. To catch the latest Hollywood blockbuster, you went to the movie theatre or a video-rental outlet. And so on. This made for a lot of walking, even if you took your car or public transport to cover most of the distance.

The same thing applied at work. To copy a document, you walked over to the photocopier. To send a message, you walked across to the fax machine. To check last quarter's sales figures, you walked to the filing cabinet where the documentation was kept and physically leafed through the pages. To ask questions or get information from your colleagues, you walked to their offices and actually spoke to them.

Taken individually, these seemingly insignificant body movements might seem trivial; but over the course of the day, they added up to highly beneficial physical exercise.

Not for nothing are today's sedentary office workers advised by doctors to get up from their desks every hour for a five-minute break. This is apparently even better than getting up only once at the end of two hours for a 10-minute break. Research has shown that sitting for extensive periods is linked to a long list of everyday health problems – and also to a higher risk of heart disease, cancer and even early death. What little time that would have been spent walking or moving around outside has been further reduced, even eliminated. And Covid lockdowns only worsened the situation by keeping people indoors. The human body is designed for activity and movement. Who knew?

The computer and the smartphone have literally glued us to our seats, effectively removing the natural physical movements that were once part of everyday life. The internet has, in a sense, become the ultimate labour-saving device, radically reducing the need to keep our bodies moving.

It's no exaggeration to say that the only utilitarian reason people need to get up from their seats these days is to get something to eat or drink, or to go to the bathroom.

In his book, *Primate Change*, author Vybarr Cregan-Reid raises the possibility that our sedentary lifestyles may actually be changing our bodies. In an article in *The Guardian* entitled "Why exercise alone won't save us", he argues that physical activity needs to be a part of our everyday lives, rather than something that is left for the gym.

Even the gym itself is a fairly recent phenomenon. When I first started work in the 1980s, it wasn't even a part of workplace vocabulary. If you left the office and told your colleagues you were going to gym, they probably would have assumed you were training for some competitive event. Of course, people did exercise back then to keep fit. They played sport in the evening or on weekends, or they went jogging or swimming. But the notion of going to a purpose-built health facility kitted out with fitness machines and a lap-pool would have seemed strange.

It was only really in the 1990s that it took off as a mass-market phenomenon on the back of a growing worldwide fitness trend. Today, gyms and health clubs are almost as ubiquitous as supermarket chains.

It's unclear whether this fitness boom was triggered by the increasingly sedentary nature of the workplace, or whether it evolved naturally alongside as a broader societal phenomenon. Either way, gyms and health clubs arrived at the precise time when we needed them most. After spending most of the working day on our butts staring at a screen, even a short half-hour workout afterwards feels like a treat.

Everyday physical activity has evolved from something you did naturally without even being aware of it, to something you consciously have to make time for. How strange.

IN CLOSING

Chapter 30

Technostalgia

All the warm, nostalgic memories of life before the internet that you've read in this book may come across as one man's hopeless, unrealistic harking back to a lost era. But business is also jumping onto the pre-internet nostalgia wagon, so clearly, I'm in good company.

Of course, retro-marketing, which surfs off nostalgia for another era, is nothing new. Walk into a home-appliance store and you'll see a colourful range of fridges, toasters and ovens with a distinctive retro design straight out of the 1950s and 1960s. But there's nothing retro about their performance, as they all boast the reliability and technology of today.

Out on the roads, you'll see the modern-day incarnations of classic cars like the Mini, the VW Beetle and the Fiat 500. They're all bigger and more spacious than their 1960s forebears, have modern-day engines and are technologically loaded with all the bells and whistles.

Traditional retro-marketing is therefore all about new wine in old bottles. In other words, you're still doing all the things that modern technology allows, but in an emotionally packaged retro design.

Over the past five years, however, we've seen a new wave of retro-marketing, one associated with the era before the internet when life was much simpler. Except that these are new products and services that have been *intentionally* simplified and slowed down. This "technostalgia" has shown up in cell phones, music and cameras – ironically, the very areas that have seen the greatest technological progress thanks to the internet.

How can this be? There have been many attempts at explaining this curious phenomenon. They all revolve around lifestyle and taking back control. Cue buzzwords like slow living and a return to a simpler way of life.

Take ordinary cell phones (or dumbphones, the forebears of smartphones). They handle just two things: phone calls and text messaging; and their battery life is measured in days rather than hours. Optional extras include a basic internet connection, a camera and a couple of games. Fully loaded has never seemed so light.

Interestingly, it's not just children, seniors and people in developing countries who are buying these phones; they're also proving to be a useful second device for smartphone owners desperate for some downtime from the pressures of being constantly connected. You can now actually leave your smartphone at home, knowing that you are still reachable.

Music has also seen a return to the old days, with vinyl records and turntables making a comeback. Today, you have ready access to online music libraries with nearly 100 million songs, so why would you want to go back to a few records that sit on a shelf? Never mind the fact that to play a record, you have to manually remove it from its jacket, load it onto the turntable and then gently lower the stylus onto the surface. Go figure.

Photography has seen a similar transition from fast to slow that defies logical explanation. Like in the old days, you can now once again buy a reflex camera that requires photos to be developed in a photo-processing lab. You must really want to make a statement when you elect to set aside smartphone point-and-click photography with its immediate results, in favour of a costly, time-consuming manual process built around a bulky device that you can't even slip into your pocket.

There is even a new smartphone photo app called Dispo (as in Disposable Camera) which intentionally downgrades the capability of your camera-phone. There are no fancy features like filters, editing or text. Your photos are digitally "developed" and delivered the next day. Dispo is the antithesis of Instagram, because it favours slow and simple over instant gratification and the pursuit of the impossibly perfect picture. Also, when a photo requires time to get right and comes at a cost, you put a lot more thought and effort into it. Holding the finished picture in your hand days later has a certain emotional value that a digital picture cannot always match.

Interestingly, many of the people who are into this kind of technostalgia are digital natives themselves. They seem to feel a need to slow down and simplify things. After all, why else would you want to spend *more* time and effort doing something, for an outcome that is technologically inferior to its digital equivalent? Could it reflect a certain disillusionment with some aspects of the internet?

For some people at least, there seems to be a new way of doing things; it's called the old way.

Chapter 31

Off the grid in Mexico

I was struggling to write a suitable ending for this book when my 25-year-old son serendipitously came to the rescue. He relates how he survived a backpacking trip in Mexico without internet access for much of the time. It is very instructive, and ties back neatly to many of the themes in the book. Here is his story.

"After completing my university studies in France, I decided to take a break before starting to look for my first job. I opted for a backpacking trip across Mexico, where I had done a university exchange programme a year earlier.

Besides wanting to discover more of the country, I wanted to travel by myself and get out of my comfort zone. I needed to think about what I really wanted to do in life, and I thought that there was no better way to know yourself than to be by yourself.

So, I left on a one-month cross-country trip, starting in Playa del Carmen. I knew more or less where I wanted to go, so I started by working my way across the Yucatan peninsula by bus. From there, I flew to Chiapas, where I spent most of the time in the tropical rainforests, far off the beaten track. I then took a plane to Oaxaca, where I spent some time in Puerto Escondido and Chacahua. I had no pre-arranged itinerary, and decided when and where to stay as I went along.

I often found myself in remote towns and villages. Some had no roads; others were only accessible by boat. There was little or no internet access – and sometimes not even an ATM. After the fully connected life that I had just left behind in Paris, it was a bit intimidating to suddenly find myself off the grid. I did not know anybody. I was unable to reach out to my friends online. I'm not a big user of social media, but it had always been reassuring to be able to contact them with just a few clicks. I gradually realized to what extent my phone had been an integral part of my comfort zone – always there when I needed it. But the hardest part wasn't the social isolation; it was learning how to pass the time and stay entertained without the internet!

I soon had to talk to people, more out of necessity than choice. This was my big 'aha!' moment, especially as I am not a natural extrovert. I had to put aside this reserved aspect of my personality and force myself to talk to people. It was often the only way to find a place to eat, or somewhere to spend the night. These encounters allowed me to experience the pleasure of connecting with others on a personal level.

Yes, the internet allows us to do lots of wonderful things on holiday, from finding our way around to discovering tourist attractions and restaurants. But you can also just stop and ask people in the street, or trust your instincts and try out different places. Sure, you might end up disappointed, but that's life. And at least you don't have to give any ratings afterwards!

Reduced internet access also allowed me to reconnect with myself and learn to appreciate the value of idle time. I found myself in some really beautiful parts of the country. I read books, walked and contemplated nature. How different this was from our everyday lives. As soon as we have a free moment, we pick up our phones. It's a quick fix that prevents us from using our imagination, contemplating things or simply reflecting.

Being off the grid ended up being a very enriching experience. Without the constant distraction of the internet, I felt I was living more intensely and authentically. It was all the more so as everyone was in the same boat in terms of lack of internet access. We all had the same mindset. Speaking to others face-to-face was the default mode of social interaction, rather than something exceptional or unusual.

When I got back to Paris after my trip, I reconnected with my circle of friends, with whom I am very close. When we are together, we talk a lot and also play board games and cards, which allows me to spend less time online. It made me realize how hooked on the internet our generation is. We grew up with it. It has assumed such proportions that we can feel lost without it. When people say they're not hooked on the internet, just drop them in a strange place with no network and see how they manage. I've been there!

That said, it's not possible – or even desirable – to disconnect completely from the internet. After all, it remains an integral part of our lives. But one can try and spend less time on it. I'd like to think I've achieved a reasonable balance."

APPENDIX

The internet made simple

If you search online for a definition of the internet, the chances are that the very first sentence will contain words like *interconnected computers, protocols, architecture* and *network* – even *network of networks*. Needless to say, such definitions are incomprehensible to the average person because they don't relate to everyday life.

It would be like defining a car in terms of engines, pistons, fuel injection and gearboxes, whereas a more understandable definition of a car might be "an engine-powered passenger vehicle that anyone can learn to drive, and which you can use for your everyday activities, from shopping to taking the children to school".

Let us now take a look at what the internet is and how it came about.

Information sharing through the ages

Put simply, the internet is nothing more than the latest chapter in the history of information-sharing. Since the dawn of humanity, people have needed to share information with others who were some distance away, often in another village or town. They might send a man on foot or on horseback to deliver a message verbally. Alternatively, they might communicate by beating a drum, sending smoke signals or reflecting the sun off a mirror.

With the advent of writing and paper, information-sharing took a great leap forward because the messenger no longer needed to know the content of the message being carried; it could be sealed and delivered confidentially. In fact, medieval riders on horseback were essentially the forerunners of what was eventually to become courier services, and finally the venerable Post Office itself.

From the Middle Ages through to the late 20th century, the technology might have changed (horse, carriage, ship, carrier-pigeon, van, train, plane) but the concept remained the same: information written on paper had to be physically transported from point A to point B.

The telegraph, the telephone and the fax machine speeded the process up considerably. However, there was only so much you could say in dots and dashes, or over the phone with the meter running. Letters and paper documents therefore remained the lifeblood of communities and organizations, which were 100% dependent on postal services. Even with the arrival of the computer age in the 1960s, digitally stored information still needed to be transformed into paper documents before it could be used – for example, an airline ticket or a phone bill.

In summary, virtually all forms of information-sharing before the arrival of the internet involved the production, distribution and storage of paper in one form of another. The internet changed all that because it enabled information-sharing to be "dematerialized". This was a completely new paradigm.

The end of the paper trail

How could something as fundamental as paper, on which humanity had relied for centuries, no longer be required for communication?

The trick was to convert human language into computer language – more specifically, into a digital format consisting of bits and bytes (binary 0s and 1s). The digitally transformed letters and words could now be stored electronically and took up a lot less space; an entire book could fit onto a microchip the size of your thumbnail. These digital bits and bytes were also able to travel at a phenomenal speed that the Post Office could never match, because they moved electronically.

But there was still something missing. You still had to figure out a way to display the information at the other end for people to read. You needed an affordable electronic device that people could use in schools, libraries, cafés and even at home. This device was the personal computer. It closed the loop and enabled the complete replacement of paper. Information could now be produced and transported – *and* displayed electronically at the other end. It no longer needed to be printed.

It wasn't long before sound, pictures and even film were being transformed into digital format. Dematerialized information expanded beyond writing to include voice, images and video. It was all stored in the same digital language of 0s and 1s.

The scene was now set for the concept of an internet.

A universal filing cabinet

The internet can be viewed as a universal filing system. It gathers information, stores it in digital form, and then shares it with people on their phones and computers.

This information can be literally anything, from the trivial (a picture of your dog's breakfast) and the useful (an educational video) to the important (the results of your Covid test). If there's a market for it, it will find its way onto the internet.

All of these different forms of information – text, audio, images – are stored digitally in remote data centres around the world. These are air-conditioned, warehouse-like buildings that hold vast banks of interconnected computers and storage servers. Data centres can use as much electricity as a small town.

This digital information is then shared online with people around the world on affordable devices like laptops, tablets and smartphones, using a web browser or an app.

Cutting out the middleman

Before the internet, you needed an intermediary to be able to share information on paper. The quintessential example was the Post Office, which transported letters from one location to another. Another might be the official standing behind the counter at, say, the Motor Vehicle Department, who collects your driver's licence application and passes it on for further processing.

But today, you can do all of this yourself. Instead of sending a letter through the Post Office, you can just send an email. Instead of standing in line at the Motor Vehicle Department, you can apply for your driver's licence online. You can bank, shop and pay your taxes from the comfort of your armchair. The paper trail of forms, letters and documents that used to take days or weeks moving between departments has now been replaced by a few minutes online at your computer.

Economists call this "disintermediation", which is the removal of intermediaries, or middlemen, between producers and consumers. It is probably one of the most fundamental everyday benefits of the internet.

Head in the clouds

The information stored in data centres is often referred to as residing "in the cloud". That's another way of saying that the information is stored somewhere out there. Where exactly, you don't really know, and probably don't even care. It's a bit like electricity; you don't know or care which power station it comes from, as long as it's there when you need it.

Internet services are either free (in exchange for your personal information and browsing behaviour, often unbeknownst to you) or paid for, depending on the business model of the company providing the service.

Another thing about the internet is that it doesn't belong to any person, organization or government. Anyone, from a ten-year-old schoolgirl to a billion-dollar company, can put information into it. As this book has shown, this can be a mixed blessing.

When was the internet created?

The network of interconnected computers that constitute the internet began to be assembled as far back as the mid-1980s. In those early years, it was primarily used by students and staff in universities, and by employees in technology companies in Silicon Valley. You needed to be tech-savvy to use what was still essentially "bleeding-edge" technology.

The internet only reached the general public after the creation of the World Wide Web in 1990 (by Tim Berners-Lee, since you're asking). This had the significant benefit of insulating users from the technology through easy-to-understand web pages and links. You no longer needed to be a tech-nerd to go online.

It then rapidly gained traction after the launch of the world's first commercial web browser in 1994 (Netscape Navigator), and the founding of Google in 1998. But it would take another few years before the number of internet users reached critical mass.

So, even though the internet was technically invented in the mid-1980s, it only really went mainstream at the turn of the century, around the year 2000.

Better late than never

Why did it take so long for the internet to arrive? After all, huge mainframe computers were in general use since the 1960s, and personal computers since the 1980s. There were two reasons for this.

Firstly, these early computers were clunky, horrendously expensive and essentially used for number-crunching – i.e., calculations. Secondly, disk storage and memory were very expensive. In the 1960s, 1 MB (megabyte) of disk storage could cost a million dollars; today, it costs only a few cents.

It would take another thirty years of technological progress before computers became small and powerful enough, and storage cheap enough, to enable the internet to emerge. Today, the $100 smartphone in your pocket is exponentially more powerful, and contains far more memory and storage, than the mainframes of the 1960s and the personal computers of the 1980s. Storage is now so cheap that a lot of it is given away; for barely a dollar per month, you can top up with another 50MB.

The web vs the internet

For convenience, we often use the terms web and internet interchangeably. In reality, the internet is the network of interconnected computers that store the information (i.e., the filing system), while the web is the collection of information that you access using your browser. An analogy would be a bookshop or library (the internet), which contains books (the web) where the information is stored.

Biography

Michael Gentle is a former IT and data-privacy professional. He has worked in software development, project management and marketing in global companies such as Apple, The Bank of Tokyo and the Nestlé group.

He studied mechanical engineering, aeronautical engineering and information technology, and is the author of a number of best-selling books in business and technology.

He has lived and worked in Europe, North America, Africa and Asia-Pacific, and speaks several languages. He is now retired in Portugal.

Note to Reader

If you enjoyed this snapshot of life before the internet and would like to learn more, then please visit my website at www. lifebeforetheinternet.com.

References

BOOKS

1. Harris, M. (2015) *The End of Absence: Reclaiming What We've Lost in a World of Constant Connection*, New York, Penguin.
2. Skenazy, L. (2021) *Free-Range Kids: How Parents and Teachers Can Let Go and Let Grow*, Hoboken, Jossey-Bass.

ARTICLES

3. Cregan-Reid, V. (2019) "Why exercise alone won't save us", *The Guardian*, 3 January [Online]. Available at https://www.theguardian.com/news/2019/jan/03/why-exercise-alone-wont-save-us
4. *Future of Earth* (2017) "Poor Numeracy Hits Workplace Productivity", 7 July [Online]. Available at https://futureofearth.online/poor-numeracy-can-hit-workplace-productivity/
5. Lu, D. "Clarke's Three Laws", *New Scientist* [Online]. Available at https://www.newscientist.com/definition/clarkes-three-laws/
6. *Statista* (2020) "Percentage of households with landline telephones in the United Kingdom (UK) from 1970 to 2018", 7 December [Online]. Available at https://www.statista.com/statistics/289158/telephone-presence-in-households-in-the-uk/
7. *Time* (1979) "Press: Whip His What?", 25 June [Online]. Available at https://content.time.com/time/subscriber/article/0,33009,912465,00.html
8. Zagorsky, J.L. (2019) "Rise and fall of the landline: 143 years of telephones becoming more accessible – and smart", *The Conversation*, 14 March [Online]. Available at https://theconversation.com/rise-and-fall-of-the-landline-143-

years-of-telephones-becoming-more-accessible-and-smart-113295

QUOTES

9. *Quotepark* (2021) "It's tough to make predictions, especially about the future [Online]. Available at https://quotepark. com/quotes/1200889-yogi-berra-its-tough-to-make-predictions-especially-about-t/

Further Reading

BOOKS

1. Carr, N. (2011) *The Shallows: What the Internet Is Doing to Our Brains*, New York, W.W. Norton & Company.
2. Desmurget, M. (2019) *La fabrique du crétin digital (The digital cretin factory)*, Paris, Points.
3. Newport, C. (2021) *A World Without Email: Reimagining Work in an Age of Communication Overload*, New York, Portfolio Penguin.
4. Nichols, T. (2017) *The Death of Expertise: The Campaign against Established Knowledge and Why it Matters*, New York, Oxford University Press USA.
5. Skenazy, L. (2021) *Free-Range Kids: How Parents and Teachers Can Let Go and Let Grow*, Hoboken, Jossey-Bass.
6. Steiner-Adair, C. and Barker, T.H. (2013) *The Big Disconnect: Protecting Childhood and Family Relationships in the Digital Age*, New York, Harper.
7. Turkle, S. (2012) *Alone Together: Why We Expect More from Technology and Less from Each Other*, New York, Basic Books.
8. Turkle, S. (2015) *Reclaiming Conversation: The Power of Talk in a Digital Age*, New York, Penguin.
9. Wolf, M. (2018) *Reader, Come Home: The Reading Brain in a Digital World*, New York, Harper.

ARTICLES

10. Bergland, C. (2020) "Why Cursive Handwriting Is Good for Your Brain", *Psychology Today*, 2 October [Online]. Available at https://www.psychologytoday.com/us/blog/the-athletes-way/202010/why-cursive-handwriting-is-good-your-brain

11. *Children and Screens* (2017) "Obesity", 1 November [Online]. Available at https://www.childrenandscreens.com/findings/obesity/

12. Harford, T. (2022) "Your phone's notification settings and the meaning of life", *The Financial Times*, 24 June [Online]. Available at https://www.ft.com/content/88ea6172-cbff-4c68-8ec8-32f0884fc6a5

13. McLaren, L. (2019) "Innocence lost: what did you do before the internet?", *The Guardian*, 4 August [Online]. Available at https://www.theguardian.com/technology/2019/aug/04/innocence-lost-what-did-you-do-before-the-internet

14. *OSF HealthCare* (2020) "Screen Time for Kids; How Much is Too Much?", 10 January [Online]. Available at https://newsroom.osfhealthcare.org/screen-time-for-kids-how-much-is-too-much/

15. Pring, B. (2021) "We owe it to our kids to put an age limit on social media", *Techcrunch*, 25 May [Online]. Available at https://techcrunch.com/2021/05/25/we-owe-it-to-our-kids-to-put-an-age-limit-on-social-media/

FILMS and DOCUMENTARIES

16. *Chasing Childhood* (2021) Directed by Margaret Munzer Loeb and Eden Wurmfeld [Film]. New York.

17. *The Social Dilemma* (2020) Directed by Jeff Orlowski [Film]. Exposure Labs.

WEBSITES

18. Center for Humane Technology, https://www.humanetech.com/

19. Free-Range Kids, https://www.freerangekids.com/

20. Let Grow, https://letgrow.org/

21. The Social Dilemma, www.thesocialdilemma.com

O-BOOKS

SPIRITUALITY

O is a symbol of the world, of oneness and unity; this eye represents knowledge and insight. We publish titles on general spirituality and living a spiritual life. We aim to inform and help you on your own journey in this life.
If you have enjoyed this book, why not tell other readers by posting a review on your preferred book site?

Recent bestsellers from O-Books are:

Heart of Tantric Sex

Diana Richardson
Revealing Eastern secrets of deep love and intimacy to Western couples.
Paperback: 978-1-90381-637-0 ebook: 978-1-84694-637-0

Crystal Prescriptions

The A-Z guide to over 1,200 symptoms and their healing crystals
Judy Hall
The first in the popular series of eight books, this handy little guide is packed as tight as a pill-bottle with crystal remedies for ailments.
Paperback: 978-1-90504-740-6 ebook: 978-1-84694-629-5

Take Me To Truth
Undoing the Ego
Nouk Sanchez, Tomas Vieira
The best-selling step-by-step book on shedding the Ego, using the
teachings of *A Course In Miracles*.
Paperback: 978-1-84694-050-7 ebook: 978-1-84694-654-7

The 7 Myths about Love...Actually!
The Journey from your HEAD to the HEART of your SOUL
Mike George
Smashes all the myths about LOVE.
Paperback: 978-1-84694-288-4 ebook: 978-1-84694-682-0

The Holy Spirit's Interpretation of the New Testament
A Course in Understanding and Acceptance
Regina Dawn Akers
Following on from the strength of *A Course In Miracles*, NTI
teaches us how to experience the love and oneness of God.
Paperback: 978-1-84694-085-9 ebook: 978-1-78099-083-5

The Message of A Course In Miracles
A translation of the Text in plain language
Elizabeth A. Cronkhite
A translation of *A Course In Miracles* into plain, everyday
language for anyone seeking inner peace. The companion
volume, *Practicing A Course In Miracles*, offers practical lessons
and mentoring.
Paperback: 978-1-84694-319-5 ebook: 978-1-84694-642-4

Your Simple Path
Find Happiness in every step
Ian Tucker
A guide to helping us reconnect with what is really important in our lives.
Paperback: 978-1-78279-349-6 ebook: 978-1-78279-348-9

365 Days of Wisdom
Daily Messages To Inspire You Through The Year
Dadi Janki
Daily messages which cool the mind, warm the heart and guide you along your journey.
Paperback: 978-1-84694-863-3 ebook: 978-1-84694-864-0

Body of Wisdom
Women's Spiritual Power and How it Serves
Hilary Hart
Bringing together the dreams and experiences of women across the world with today's most visionary spiritual teachers.
Paperback: 978-1-78099-696-7 ebook: 978-1-78099-695-0

Dying to Be Free
From Enforced Secrecy to Near Death to True Transformation
Hannah Robinson
After an unexpected accident and near-death experience, Hannah Robinson found herself radically transforming her life, while a remarkable new insight altered her relationship with her father, a practising Catholic priest.
Paperback: 978-1-78535-254-6 ebook: 978-1-78535-255-3

The Ecology of the Soul
A Manual of Peace, Power and Personal Growth for Real People
in the Real World
Aidan Walker
Balance your own inner Ecology of the Soul to regain your
natural state of peace, power and wellbeing.
Paperback: 978-1-78279-850-7 ebook: 978-1-78279-849-1

Not I, Not other than I
The Life and Teachings of Russel Williams
Steve Taylor, Russel Williams
The miraculous life and inspiring teachings of one of the World's
greatest living Sages.
Paperback: 978-1-78279-729-6 ebook: 978-1-78279-728-9

On the Other Side of Love
A woman's unconventional journey towards wisdom
Muriel Maufroy
When life has lost all meaning, what do you do?
Paperback: 978-1-78535-281-2 ebook: 978-1-78535-282-9

Practicing A Course In Miracles
A translation of the Workbook in plain language, with
mentor's notes
Elizabeth A. Cronkhite
The practical second and third volumes of The Plain-Language
A Course In Miracles.
Paperback: 978-1-84694-403-1 ebook: 978-1-78099-072-9

Quantum Bliss

The Quantum Mechanics of Happiness, Abundance, and Health

George S. Mentz

Quantum Bliss is the breakthrough summary of success and spirituality secrets that customers have been waiting for.

Paperback: 978-1-78535-203-4 ebook: 978-1-78535-204-1

The Upside Down Mountain

Mags MacKean

A must-read for anyone weary of chasing success and happiness – one woman's inspirational journey swapping the uphill slog for the downhill slope.

Paperback: 978-1-78535-171-6 ebook: 978-1-78535-172-3

Your Personal Tuning Fork

The Endocrine System

Deborah Bates

Discover your body's health secret, the endocrine system, and 'twang' your way to sustainable health!

Paperback: 978-1-84694-503-8 ebook: 978-1-78099-697-4

Readers of ebooks can buy or view any of these bestsellers by clicking on the live link in the title. Most titles are published in paperback and as an ebook. Paperbacks are available in traditional bookshops. Both print and ebook formats are available online.

Find more titles and sign up to our readers' newsletter at http://www.johnhuntpublishing.com/mind-body-spirit

Follow us on Facebook at https://www.facebook.com/OBooks/ and Twitter at https://twitter.com/obooks